The Hakomi Way
Consciousness & Healing
The Legacy of Ron Kurtz

Author :
Ron Kurtz
1934 - 2011

Contributors:
Donna Martin & Georgia Marvin

Editors:
**Georgia Marvin, Caroline Braham,
Sophie Cattier, Trudy Johnston**

Copyright © 2018 by Ron Kurtz

All rights reserved. No portion of this book may be reproduced, stored in a retrieval system, or transmitted in any form or by any means – electronic, mechanical, photocopy, recording, scanning, internet or other – except for brief quotations in critical reviews or articles, without the prior written permission of the copyright holder. For permission requests contact the estate of Ron Kurtz through www.hakomi.com

ISBN-13: 978-1987529654
ISBN-10: 1987529650

Contributors: Donna Martin and Georgia Marvin
Editors: Georgia Marvin, Caroline Braham, Sophie Cattier, Trudy Johnston

Graphic Art Work: Cover and Interior Layout by Sue Reynolds,
www.piquantproductions.ca

Cover Image: Vector art from bigstockphoto.com
Artist: Denis Krivoy

Published by Stone's Throw Publications   www.stonesthrowps.ca
13240 Mast Road, Port Perry, ON L9L 1B5   Canada

Printed and distributed by CreateSpace.com, a division of Amazon.com

Visit **Ron Kurtz Hakomi Educational Materials**
www.hakomi.com

9 8 7 6 5 4 3 2 1

"A good therapist, shares control with everything present, sometimes moving deeply into the unfolding action, sometimes waiting quietly as the other does inner work, surfing gracefully the changing amplitudes of intimacy." ~ Ron Kurtz

Table of Contents

Foreword — 1

Preface — 3

Introduction — 5
   A Little History — 7
   Some Essential Aspects of the Method — 11
   Loving Presence and The Hakomi Principles — 15

The Method — 17
   A Brief Overview — 19
   The Hakomi Way — 23

The Nature of Mind and Brain — 29
   States of Consciousness — 31
   Consciousness as Choice — 33
   Consciousness is Limited — 35
   Becoming Conscious of What? — 36
   The Unconscious: Self-States — 40
   The Amazing Case for How Unconscious We Are — 42
   The Adaptive Unconscious — 47
   The Nature of Belief — 58
   Implicit Beliefs and Rules — 61

Mindfulness in Hakomi — 67
   The Client's Commitments: Mindfulness and Honesty — 69
   The Focus on Present Experience — 71
   How the Mind Makes Meaning — 73
   History of Mindfulness Practice — 75
   What Mindfulness Is — 75
   How to Become Mindful — 78
   How Mindfulness is Used in Evoking Reactions — 79
   How to Study and Report Your Reactions — 81
   Musings on the Self - What are We Observing? — 81

Loving Presence — 85
- The Therapist's State of Mind — 87
- Loving Presence — 90

Contact and tracking — 95
- Contact — 95
- Tracking - The Steps: Where Attention Goes — 103

Indicators — 107
- Working with Indicators — 110
- Shifting Your Own Attention — 111
- Shifting the Client's Attention to the Indicator — 112
- Indicators as Data for Experiments — 114
- Nonverbal Indicators and Formative Experiences — 116
- Examples of Indicators — 118

Experiments — 119
- Experiments 1st Essay — 121
- Experiments 2nd Essay — 122
- Taking Over — 128

Healing and Missing Experiences — 133
- The Healing Process — 135
- The Healing Relationship — 138
- The Right State of Mind — 140
- Stewardship — 141
- The Natural Course of Healing — 144
- Missing Experiences — 146
- What is Missing? — 148
- Integration — 151

Process and Structure — 153
- An Outline of the Method — 155
- Guidelines for the Way Things Work — 161
- The Process As Three Phases — 170
- The Process as Six Skill Sets — 178
- The Process in Graphic Form — 182
- Logic of the Method — 183

Skillful Hakomi — 185
    The Dance — 187
    On Being A Portal — 191
    Silence & Following — 194
    Moving the Process Forward — 197
    Habits as Causes of Failure — 197

Refinements — 205
    Original Components, (Kurtz 1997) — 207
    The Major Refinements (Kurtz 2010) — 210
    Talks on Refined Hakomi — 214
    Hakomi Simplified — 231
    Ten Basic Elements of the Refined Method — 233

Bibliography — 243

To my beloved wife, Terry Toth

For one human being to love another; that is perhaps the most difficult of all our tasks, the ultimate, the last test and proof the work for which all other work is but preparation.
(Rilke, 1929)

With you my love, it was easy.

Foreword

Ron Kurtz died on January 4, 2011. For many of us, he was the original authority on Hakomi. He left a legacy of teachings and materials, hard drives and videos. As many of you know, he distributed his materials widely and freely in order for as many people to have access to Hakomi as possible. In 2017, his wife, Terry Toth, began an ambitious archival project to save and eventually curate his collections of writings, digital files, videos and audio recordings. Eventually the entirety of his work will be available to students of the method, to his teachers and trainers and to academic researchers.

Before he died, he had produced a training manual for his students and many abridged versions of that manual were distributed to workshop participants around the world. The last version of the Training Handbook for the Refined Hakomi Method was published in 2011 and made available on his website, hakomi.com. My attempt at editing that publication was limited both by my desire not to disturb his voice or his message and by the complexity of the project. I was not willing to expand on his point form notes about healing or complexity theory or to offer a version of his ideas without his authorization. For those of you whom he taught, you will remember that he talked about love and stars and eternity. It is difficult to capture his vast thinking and certainly impossible to summarize it.

It has now been six years since his death and his trainers have been asking for a better version of the manual, one that retains the vitality and authenticity of his voice but one that also matches the pedagogy and curriculum of the Hakomi Education Network training teams. This edited version is an attempt to bring together his thoughts

Foreword

and his writings in one manual, his last word on the subject of Hakomi and how he wanted it to be taught and practiced after he was gone.

Because Ron was unable to publish his final thoughts on Hakomi before he died, we have attempted to collate his thoughts on the subject under one title: *The Hakomi Way: Consciousness and Healing, 2018.* These writings are a compilation of transcribed talks given to international training groups, his previously published ideas on various subjects, expansion of point form notes into prose, and expanded discussions of some of his ideas.

The team that has collaborated on this legacy project consists of four of his international trainers: Georgia Marvin, Caroline Braham, Sophie Cattier and Trudy Johnston. I would like to thank them for the countless hours they have spent reading and editing and discussing Ron's work. The project grew out of a Hakomi Education Network gathering in the early spring of 2016 in Puerto Morelos, Mexico. Our hope is that it keeps Ron's voice alive in the midst of the learning and that it contributes to his great legacy.

Georgia Marvin
British Columbia, Canada

Preface

It has been thirty-six years since I began to develop the Hakomi Method. At present, it is being taught by dozens of people in fifteen countries. During those years the work has evolved quite a bit. A few major changes and many lesser ones have been made. This document describes the work as I teach it now, in 2011. The latest version is a significant refinement of the original. Some important things have been added, others that now seem unnecessary have been dropped.

The work from the beginning was experiential, focused on the present and using reactions evoked by little experiments with a person in a mindful state. Those experiments remain the core of the method.

Sixteen years ago, I introduced the idea that loving presence is the appropriate state of mind for the practitioner. I made it the first and most important task. That one change made a huge difference in the effectiveness of the method.

More recently and equally significant, I came to see the work as assisted self-study. This view is quite different from that of traditional psychotherapy. I see it now as *mindfulness-based, assisted self study*.

Seen in this light, it is closely related to the Buddhist and Taoist principles that were among my original inspirations. As assisted self-study, the work is, in some fundamental way, quite different from those therapies that find their foundations in medicine and place themselves within that paradigm. This method can be part of any method of psychotherapy. But it is much more than that. It is basic to all human relations. It is a natural part of the universal human endeavor to understand ourselves, to free ourselves of the inevitable suffering that

Preface

follows from ignorance of who we are and "how the world hangs together". It is the path taken by all who work to go beyond the half-remembered hurts and failed beliefs that linger unexamined in the mind and body, hurts that act through barely conscious habits and reactions. This work is a part of that heroic labor, a cousin to sitting meditation, to singing bowls and chanting monks.

Anyone who is capable of a few moments of calm will have no trouble pursuing self-study using this method. And just as exciting, assisting in that process is well within the reach of any good-hearted, intelligent person who takes the time to learn the method.

A word of appreciation. In practicing, learning and teaching all these years, I have benefited greatly from the people I have assisted, the colleagues I have worked with, and all the bright and loving students who have been a big part of my life. To all of them, I offer heartfelt thanks!

Ron Kurtz
Ashland, Oregon
January, 2010

Introduction

In order to create a connected narrative as a guide to readers, we have introduced each section with a brief explanation of its source or its relation to the whole. You will notice that some of the writing is Ron's voice in present tense, as if he were still alive. Some of the writing has been expanded and we refer to him in past tense. Our hope is that his voice and his thinking remain vivid for all of his readers and students.

> Ron wrote this article in 2010 to explain how he understood his refined method.

A Little History

I'd like to clear up some of the confusion concerning what the Hakomi method is and what it means to teach it. Hakomi is a word that came in a dream to one of my earliest students, David Winter. In that dream I handed him a piece of paper that had the words Hakomi Therapy on it. At the time, a few of us had been searching for a name for the work I had developed. We found out that the word Hakomi meant "How do you stand in relation to these many realms" or "Who are you?" in the Hopi language. It seemed very appropriate and, because it came in a dream to someone who had no idea what it meant, we adopted it.

Early in the 1970's, I began to create the techniques and ideas that eventually became the Hakomi Method. I developed little experiments done with the client in a mindful state, experiments like verbal experiments. These experiments were done to evoke informative reactions and emotional healing processes. Probes were one kind of such experiments. I also began supporting spontaneous management behaviors by "taking over" the behavior. I took over tensions, voices, holding back and other spontaneous reactions. Tracking and contact were also developed then.

During the 70's, I first outlined the linear process. In the early 1980's, the principles were developed with the help of students and co-leaders. This whole body of ideas and techniques became the original Hakomi Method. I, and others, taught it that way all through the 80's. Late in that decade, I discovered loving presence and began teaching it as an important part of the method. I left the Hakomi Institute in the late 80's and continued teaching as a separate entity, Ron Kurtz Trainings, Inc. Since that time, my vision of the Method has continued to evolve.

Introduction

In my approach, the method has always been malleable and generative of new ideas. Early on, when someone in a training would ask, "How do you "do" Hakomi?" I used to say, "I'm not trying to *do* Hakomi; Hakomi is trying to do me." This was years ago and back then it was the truth. The work that came to be called Hakomi was almost completely my creation.

During all the years since I began, I've never viewed Hakomi as something fixed and rigid. I've always and only been doing what inspired me, adding new ideas which came frequently. I've always and only been trying to express what delighted my mind and touched my heart. Happily, I have been blessed with frequent inspirations. I have read a lot and have worked with many people, in many different countries. I've enjoyed the company of poets, spiritual teachers and scientists. I have known and had support from many, many loving, bright and generous people. All of them have added to my life and the development of the method.

Once, during the Q&A period after a talk, a woman asked me how I developed the Hakomi method. Recalling that Isaac Newton said, "If I have seen a little further it is by standing on the shoulders of giants." I told the audience, "I stand with my hands in the pockets of giants." It was a joke and it was true. As much as anything else, I took inspiration from those pockets, the pockets of Lao Tzu and Buddha, of Meher Baba, Milton Erickson, Al Pesso, John Pierrakos and Fritz Perls, of Ben Webster, Bill Evans, Edward Hopper and Robert Frost. Every time I teach or do a session, I dip into those pockets.

I grew my own method using that inspiration, using the thousands of opportunities that came, the workshops, the trainings, the hundreds of sessions. Though I did see some great psychotherapists work, I didn't study psychotherapy formally. I cobbled together a new way of helping people, a way that is a unique and personal expression of "who I am and where I'm coming from". When I "do" it, it's not simply a method that's being applied; it is a spirit being enacted.

Over the years, that spirit has inspired others. Some of my very first students are now teachers and trainers. They loved the work enough to make it their lifelong professions. I'm happy that they did.

They have developed their own ways of "doing" it while I have continued to grow and learn and to evolve the work in my way, as they have in theirs. Since that time, we have all taken the original method in different directions.

The original version that began with me continues to be the root of all versions. Using mindfulness and experiments is still essential to all versions. The differences now are in the content of the trainings and the style of teaching. I have dropped a lot of material that I thought was no longer necessary, such as character theory and the sensitivity cycle. I no longer teach the method solely as a psychotherapy. I emphasize learning the skills through experience, practice and feedback, rather than formal lectures.

My teaching is characterized by demonstration and experiential exercises. This method is a way to help people become aware of their implicit beliefs and habits. Mine is the method of assisted self-discovery. It's for people who have the courage and capacity to discover how they became who they are. To make Hakomi effective a practitioner must be more than just someone who knows a method. The practitioner must be someone whose very presence can be healing, a person who has all the qualities needed to support emotional healing in another. My training reflects and embodies this emphasis.

I emphasize presence, warmth and kindness more than maintaining a professional demeanor. Recent research supports this emphasis on the personal qualities of the therapist. Chögyam Trungpa called it *"full human beingness"* and described the essential qualities as warmth and wakefulness (as cited in Wellwood, 1983). These are the qualities I look for in students and potential teachers. I believe that any intelligent, warm-hearted person can learn this method. I accept people into my trainings regardless of their academic background. I have taught high school students and seniors, body workers and students of Buddhism, as well as MD's, psychologists, psychiatrists and other helping professionals. They need only be motivated to wholeheartedly pursue the difficult work of understanding themselves and to help others to do the same. Happily this work is done within the warm and loving relationships the trainings foster.

Introduction

What makes the method work is the practitioner's way of being. In the same way, a trainer's way of teaching makes the trainings work. The changes I have made to the method emerged directly from my impulse to use the greatest warmth and wakefulness I can attain. The spirit I impart to the work is my own. As I grew as a practitioner and teacher, that same spirit refined the method and the teaching, until now, they are one and the same. Here in more detail is how my work evolved from its original 1980's form to the refined method I teach now in 2008.

Some Essential Aspects of the Method

I'm fairly sure that what I do is similar to what other Hakomi therapists do. Still, I began to develop and teach the work over thirty years ago. Some of my original students have themselves been teaching it for twenty-five years or more. Each of them has modified the work in some ways. I certainly have. Still, the most essential elements have changed little. Those elements are what this paper is about.

Though based on the best science available, the method is not only science. The intimate and delicate exchanges the work gives rise to can be as beautiful as poetry or song. The skills needed are as much those of the heart as of the head. As science, the method is reason, rules and tools. The use of these, however, is an art. As in any art, there is both freedom and constraint. I am grateful for both. They have led me to whatever understanding I now enjoy. They have kept me interested and productive. They are a blessing. I also value the creativity and understanding of the other contributors to this work. And while I honor their independence and creativity, I can only write with confidence about my own vision and how I implement it.

For me, the method is a living thing. For over thirty years, my vision of the work has continuously evolved, shifting, slowly, like tectonic plates, carrying the whole endeavor. Occasionally, an earthquake of an idea radically alters my understanding. Three of these ideas were:

1. The realization of the importance of the therapist's state of mind;
2. An understanding of the method, not as working to cure disease, but as assisting another in his or her search for self-knowledge (The method can be described succinctly as: assisted self-study.)
3. An understanding of the unconscious as adaptive (Wilson, 2002), that is, intelligent, aware, working to benefit the whole

Introduction

and, without our conscious knowledge, automatically handling most of our daily actions.

"Whatever particular theory is subscribed to, all agree that expectations of other people and how they will behave are inscribed in the brain outside conscious awareness, in the period of infancy, and that they underpin our behavior in relationships through life. We are not aware of our own assumptions, but they are there, based on these earliest experiences." (Gerhardt, 2004)

The adaptive unconscious operates on the basis of assumptions, expectations, habits and implicit beliefs about ourselves, others and the world of which we are part. These assumptions were created by our earliest and strongest formative experiences. They are not available to consciousness through the usual processes that retrieve memories. They must be accessed using special techniques. The Hakomi Method employs unique techniques, developed over the past thirty plus years, to accomplish just that."

In a very real sense, we start out ignorant of who we are. To gain understanding and control requires deliberate effort. Self-study is a powerful path to change and it is most powerful when we can discover our unconscious assumptions, when we can examine them with a more mature, experienced and reasoning mind. The whole world is not the same as the limited one we spent our childhood learning to live in. To act as though it is usually results in suffering. The kinds of assumptions that cause such suffering are inaccurate, usually over-generalized, and emotionally charged. Because of this, the suffering they cause is, in principle, unnecessary. It can be lessened or even completely eliminated by changing the assumptions.

Not all formative experiences cause suffering. Positive experiences of love, protection, caring, and enjoyment can also be formative. And, of the negative ones, not all are inaccessible because they occurred too early in life. Some simply happened when the person was vulnerable. They overwhelmed the nervous system. The person simply lacked the inner resources and the external support needed to integrate them. The experiences were "encapsulated" and repressed (Rossi, 1996). The Hakomi method is designed to access these 'undigested' experiences and the habits that keep them outside of consciousness. We bring these experiences into consciousness and we find ways to integrate them. And, though the process is at times emotionally painful, it consistently accesses the adaptive unconscious. Doing so makes completion and transformation possible. And this reduces unnecessary suffering.

These ideas have reshaped my vision and the way I work. And while there have been radical shifts, some things have not changed at all or at least not very much. Though new techniques have been added, the old techniques remain central. The original underlying principles—of unity, organicity, mindfulness, mind-body wholeness and nonviolence—also remain, though my understanding and appreciation of them have deepened.

The core of the method has not changed. The essence and uniqueness of this method remains a simple combination of two things: the client's state of mind (mindfulness) and the therapist's ability to create experiments that trigger reactions while the client is in that state of mind. These reactions are indications of unconscious assumptions. These assumptions are not verbal, but are implicit in the habits which express them.

The therapist looks and listens for signs of these assumptions and tries to discern the nature of the emotionally nourishing experiences the assumptions are preventing. The therapist makes a guess about this and uses it to create an experiment that will trigger a reaction. The experiment is simply an offering of some potentially emotional nourishing statement or action, something the therapist guesses will be automatically rejected. The experiment is done while the client is in a mindful state. The client notices the reaction. The reaction, when it is allowed to unfold into an integrative process, provides an opportunity to access and examine the operations and assumptions of the adaptive unconscious that produced it. It provides

Introduction

an opportunity to complete, in a positive way, the old, painful experiences that led to those assumptions in the first place.

This simple process is the core of the method. Several other important elements of the method support this core process. These include:
1. the client's commitment and ability to enter into the process consciously and willingly
2. the therapist's ability to be present and compassionate
3. understand nonverbal expressions as signs of present experience
4. notice and understand the client's non-conscious, habitual behaviors as indicators of implicit beliefs and formative experiences
5. create experiments which will trigger reactions that can lead to emotional release and self-understanding
6. enable positive emotional experiences previously rare or entirely missing.

Loving Presence and The Hakomi Principles

Loving presence incorporates into a single concept much of what Hakomi used to present in terms of the "principles". If we briefly review the principles with respect to how each one translates into specific ways of being with the client, we'll see this...

Organicity refers to the fact that complex living systems, such as human beings, are self-organizing and self-directing. In the psychotherapeutic world, this inner thrust has been referred by Carl Rogers as the actualizing tendency. It is akin to what A. H. Almaas calls the "dynamic optimizing thrust of being".

This means that, as practitioners, we can assume there is a life-positive, self-directing, self-healing energy and intelligence at work within the client. Our task is simply to create the setting, the emotional climate that facilitates the emergence of this natural impulse toward health and to remembering wholeness.

The Principle of Mindfulness refers to the understanding that real change comes about through awareness, not efforting. When we are truly aware of our experience, when we have what Gendlin in Focusing calls the "bodily felt sense" of it, our experience naturally reveals its inherent meaning, and it continues evolving in a self-directed, life-positive direction.

As practitioners, we trust that if we can assist the client into her present-moment somatic experience, then her own awareness will facilitate whatever change or next step needs to occur.

Non-violence is being mindful of the principle and presence of organicity. It's the recognition that there is a natural way that life is unfolding, and aligning ourselves with this organic, intelligent process. As practitioners, this means we have no agendas or intentions of our own that we aren't willing to abandon at once if they somehow conflict with what is emerging from the client. It means we support the client's so-called defences (her "management behaviors"); we don't offer advice or interpretations; and we don't ask questions unless doing so serves the client.

Introduction

Holism refers to the complexity and inter-relatedness of organic systems, including human beings, with our minds and bodies, hearts and souls. It is what allows us to holographically read a person's life story in her posture or tone of voice, to infer an entire childhood from a single memory, to suspect certain core, organizing beliefs from simple repetitive gestures or words.

Unity reminds us of the inter-connectedness of all things, of all life, of all events. It is holism on a universal scale. As practitioners, unity reminds us of the ever bigger picture, of the fact that we are intimately connected to each other, and connected to our culture, our environment, our world.

As you learn the Hakomi Method, if you ground yourself in the five principles, a particular style and feel and way of being with others will naturally emerge as your way of working with clients.

Hakomi is a product of living, thinking, and feeling in terms of the principles, in alignment with the principles. In the same way, we can say that we don't have to try and learn to be in a state of loving presence. Rather, loving presence is an attitude that will naturally emerge in us as we come to deeply understand these universal spiritual principles, principles that are, in effect, the true theoretical underpinnings of Hakomi.

The Method

A Brief Overview

A good therapist shares control with everything present, sometimes moving deeply into the unfolding action, sometimes waiting quietly as the other does inner work, surfing gracefully the changing amplitudes of intimacy.

Hakomi deals with the organization of experience. For people having experiences — that's you, me and everyone else — an experience just happens, full blown and immediate. We see what we see without feeling or sensing how the brain creates images (Frith, 2007). We see the shapes and colors, we speak words and sentences, we make hundreds of movements with our eyes, all without experiencing how our brains do these things. All experience is the outcome of complex organizing processes of the brain, processes which take place outside of consciousness.

For vision, there are fifty or so different centers in the brain that contribute to the final visual experience (Crick & Koch,1995). "Are we aware of neural activity in primary visual cortex?" These centers handle things like color, depth and sequence. Their functions become obvious only when they cease to function normally.

There are some unconscious organizers that exert a very strong influence on our whole way of being. As Hakomi therapists, these are the organizers we're interested in. They are emotions, beliefs, attitudes, early learning, adaptations and memories. We call these organizers core material. Often, they are as inaccessible to ordinary consciousness as are the circuits in the brain that create vision.

However, using this method, some of them can be made conscious. The method makes core material conscious. Some core material causes unnecessary suffering and the method provides a way to reduce it. Some suffering is unnecessary because the core material that organizes it, is no longer applicable. Some beliefs, adaptations, etc. developed in early life situations no longer pertain, but are still active. Though the current situation has changed, the old adaptations are still being automatically applied. Outdated or not, they go on organizing experience, causing problems and unnecessary suffering. Of course, some suffering is normal and perhaps, necessary. Grief over a death might be an example. So, we work to bring core material into consciousness. Doing so offers the person a chance to reduce that kind of suffering. Once in consciousness, core material can be examined and revised and its influence eliminated or greatly diminished. The way we do this is unique.

We do something that no other therapy that I know of does. We do "experiments" with clients while they are in a mindful state. These experiments are brief and evocative. They are created on the basis of what we have observed about the individual and they are designed to evoke reactions that will lead directly to emotional release and/or insight. And mindfulness is essential. When a client is mindful, attention is on the flow of moment-to-moment experience. The person in a mindful state is letting things happen without trying to control them. The quality of attention is very different from ordinary attention. Attention is turned inward and just observing. In that state of being, the usual mechanisms that prevent certain thoughts and emotions are suspended. Evocative interventions at such times can produce strong, significant reactions.

Here is an example. A person who habitually talks rapidly while carefully watching his listener, may be being influenced by a core belief that people do not have time for him. Speaking rapidly is often an indicator of such a belief. One experiment the practitioner could do —with the person in a mindful state — would be to say something like this: "Please notice what happens when you hear me say, "I have time for you." That kind of statement could get a reaction, like the immediate thought, "No one ever does!" Or, the reaction could be a sudden feeling of sadness. It could be a memory of not being heard by a significant person. A whole scene like that may appear. Not just the belief is made clear. For the person noticing the reaction, the feelings and memories that arise bring with them the knowledge that this issue is still a source of emotional pain.

At this point in the process, there are things to do that will ease the hurt and modify the core material and the behaviors it is organizing. Getting to this point is what experiments in a mindful state are designed to accomplish.

Experiments in mindfulness aren't done until several other important things have happened. As a session begins, the practitioner puts him or herself into a loving state of being. (There's a lot more about this later in this document.) Loving presence is created by focusing on those qualities of the other person that inspire and support it. It is a form of attention. As we practice the method, over time this way of paying attention becomes habit. With loving presence setting the general mood, the person usually responds to it, either consciously or unconsciously, by feeling safer and calmer. The practitioner then begins to gather a particular kind of information. This information comes from observing the person's nonverbal behaviors, the kind of behaviors that are not usually focused upon.

> *"The reality of the other person is not in what he reveals to you, but in what he cannot reveal to you." (Gibran)*

The information needed for experiments is not normally gotten by asking questions or from the conversation. It's gleaned by observing behavior. At this early stage, the behaviors we're especially looking for are the signs of the person's present experience. These signs are found in posture, gestures, facial expressions and tone of voice, things like a shrug of the shoulders or a slight redness starting in the nostrils. Paying constant attention to these signs requires a kind of present awareness that needs as much practice as loving presence.

Information like this allows the practitioner to let the person know she is paying attention and is aware of what the person is feeling. It allows the practitioner to respond to the person's moods and needs before they're spoken about or even noticed by the person himself. Knowing and responding to these things without having to ask about them seems the very best way to establish intimacy and safety.

Once these are established —and it can happen within minutes —the practitioner concentrates on looking and listening not just for the signs of present experience, but for habitual nonverbal behaviors that might be the external expressions of core material, like speaking rapidly or a constant facial expression of disbelief. We call these kinds

The Method

of habits *indicators*. Indicators are usually non-conscious, meaning that they are happen automatically and without conscious awareness. They are the most fruitful subjects of experiments. Hakomi therapists are trained extensively in 'reading' nonverbal behaviors for such indicators.

When the practitioner finds an indicator to work with, she draws the person's attention to it and together they set up and do an experiment designed to bring the non-conscious organizer of that indicator into consciousness. With the person in mindfulness, the practitioner does something designed to evoke a reaction. This process brings the unconscious material closer to or into consciousness. If the practitioner has chosen a good experiment and it's done carefully with the full cooperation of the person, then a telling reaction results. The reaction itself is in consciousness because the person is in mindfulness. It is telling, because it is immediate, experiential and its connection to core material is suggested or totally obvious.

Experiments in mindfulness often evoke emotions. Emotions, when they're not interrupted, have the power to draw into consciousness, the memories and other associations that make sense of them (Damasio, 2003). Once core material is in consciousness, the work supports the expression of emotion, allowing time for the spontaneous integration that usually follows, and creating new, more realistic, and satisfying experiences and habits around the revised material. This is easier than it may sound.

To become good at this work, students and practitioners have some important things to practice. We must learn to cultivate loving presence. We must practice being loving. We must train our attention to be continuously focused on the present moment. We must learn to recognize indicators of core material. We must become good experimenters. So, we have to learn to make good guesses about what the various indicators indicate. And, we have to create experiments that will test our guesses and bring core material into consciousness. Finally, we have to be good at helping people through the painful moments that arise after experiments and to help them discover new and better ways to organize their experiences.

> Donna Martin is a long time Hakomi trainer and she was one of Ron's very closest colleagues.

The Hakomi Way

by Donna Martin

The Hakomi Method of psychotherapy was described by its creator, Ron Kurtz, as a method of mindfulness-based assisted self-discovery. What Hakomi is interested in is the organization of experience.

Experience is organized by habits, most of which are outside of conscious awareness. Some of these organizing habits create experiences of suffering, suffering which is often unnecessary. For any

The Method

real change in how we experience life in ways that are stressful or unnecessarily painful, these organizational habits, and the beliefs they are founded on, need to come into consciousness and be reviewed.

To do this, Hakomi uses mindfulness — a kind of quiet, non-interfering way of paying attention to present moment experience — and little experiments which can reveal habits and beliefs and bring them into conscious awareness. The attention in Hakomi is on present experience because we know that it reveals the organizational habits and ideas that need to be studied.

The Hakomi practitioner is trained to pay attention to two things about present experience: first, what it is (i.e. what is happening now); and second, how it is being organized. We call this way of paying attention tracking. First, we are tracking for signs of the client's present experience, especially when there is suffering. Second we are tracking for *indicators* of how experience is organized by habits and beliefs, by how the past is remembered.

We can help with the kind of suffering that is normal, like grief for the loss of a loved one. If the client's present experience is painful because of difficult life events happening in present time, we can offer compassion and comfort.

We also offer comfort when the client is experiencing emotional pain related to some past experience that has been brought to consciousness by the therapeutic work. We are mostly interested in helping the client become awake in the present moment and aware of the possibility that some kind of nourishing experience, previously missing or inaccessible, is available and possible right now.

So, in Hakomi, we are not working per se on the person's history. We are, after all, only able to guess at someone's history. Even memory is not a reliable source of information about their actual history. Remembering, however, is a present time experience and, as such, it can reveal how someone organizes experience. It is this organization of experience that we want to discover and explore as this is what causes unnecessary suffering, both in the way history is remembered as well as in present time.

The Hakomi Way is grounded in spiritual understanding from Taoism and Buddhism. Taoism teaches us that what happens is what happens. There is no should or should not about what happens or what has happened. We learn to rest into things as they are and as they are unfolding.

Buddhism teaches us about wisdom and compassion. As in Buddhism, we understand that the only reality is the present. The past is a dream. The future is a dream. Only in the present moment can we experience what is real. This realization is wisdom. However, many of us continue to experience the present as if we are in a dream. We are not fully awake to life as it is. This ignorance and delusion causes unnecessary suffering.

Present experience is organized by old habits and ideas. When the ideas that organize someone's experience are operating outside of consciousness, they are called *implicit* beliefs. When their actions are organized by behaviors that are on automatic, outside of conscious awareness, they are called *reactions*.

In Hakomi we want to assist clients to study their present experience for clues about their implicit beliefs and the habitual reactions that influence how they are organizing life experiences. We want to help clients discover new creative responses to life situations and to discover some nourishing experiences that they are not having in present time, mainly because of how they are organizing their experience.

There is some misunderstanding about what is meant by the *missing* experience in Hakomi. Let me try to clarify.

Since Hakomi is a method that focuses on present experience, even what we mean by the missing experience is something happening (or not happening) in present time. This might be related to childhood experiences, but those are outside our sphere of influence (unless we are working with an actual child). The only place where we can realistically intervene is in present time.

When the adult client seems to be recalling a childhood experience, or accessing what we might call a child part, we are still focusing on present experience. What is the person experiencing now as they are remembering? How does the person seem to be organizing his or her experience based on behaviors or ideas that are outside of conscious awareness? And what positive or nourishing experience is

The Method

missing for the person, right now, because of how she or he is organizing experience? This is what we want to help them study and explore.

Memory is one source of information about how someone is organizing experience. Nonverbal behavior is perhaps a more accurate source. Memory is a very unreliable source of accurate information about the past, but it can be a useful source of information about beliefs, especially when we pay attention to the person's behavior for indicators of those habits and beliefs connected to the narrative elicited by the memory.

Hakomi was originally referred to as body-centered psychotherapy because the information about someone's present experience and how someone is organizing experience is vastly more available from nonverbal expression than from what the person can or does say in words. So we are mainly tracking for nonverbal signs of present experience and for indicators of how the person's embodied experience is organized by unconscious habits and implicit beliefs.

In Hakomi, we observe and contact present experience to let clients know that we are following, as well as to direct their attention to their present embodied experience. And we assist them to self study by doing little experiments with those indicators as a way of bringing habits and organizing beliefs into conscious awareness.

In Hakomi, we often talk about the practitioner following. Some of what we are following constantly are signs of the client's present moment experience. We are accompanying the client on a journey to self discovery, freedom, and healing.

Sometimes we follow the client and sometimes we lead (by invitation - we invite the client to notice or study something). But we are constantly following signs of his or her present experience and how the unfolding seems to want to happen. We are following the healing energy of this journey.

The Hakomi Way has four distinguishing characteristics as a therapy method. Two have been with the method from the beginning; two evolved later. From the beginning, there was this focus on present experience and the use of little experiments in mindfulness for the purpose of self-discovery.

What has evolved is the movement toward a stronger focus on the nourishing missing experience. This evolution has been two-fold: first, there is now more understanding of the missing experience as an experience in present time. Though the missing experience may be related to the person's actual or remembered history, those memories need not be accurate to be useful.

As sources of information, reported memories, along with nonverbal behavior, can reveal a great deal about how someone unconsciously organizes experience and how this way of organizing limits them or causes unnecessary suffering. We are looking for indicators of what kind of nourishing experience the person needs now and is ready for, one that is missing only because of the person's own habits and beliefs and not because the nourishment is not available.

Secondly, we have more understanding now of how important experience is in shaping the brain, and how important the new nourishing experience is in changing how the mind perceives and responds to life. So we want to spend more time on creating the nourishing experience and less time on the old painful experience. Painful emotions are evoked only long enough to give us the information about what kind of nourishing experience is needed. The focus of attention and time in a Hakomi session is on discovering and hopefully providing the nourishing experience that is needed and making sure it is taken in, integrated, and embodied.

One way of doing this, throughout the whole therapy session, relates to the key ingredient of Hakomi as it has evolved. There has always been an awareness of the importance of what we call the healing relationship. We now realize that the key to the healing relationship is the state of mind of the therapist. We call the particular state of mind that creates the best possibility of a healing relationship loving presence. This is now recognized as the key to the whole method.

Previously, in psychotherapy generally, the therapist was supposed to be in a neutral state, somewhat emotionally detached from the client. Now the research shows that the successful therapist needs to be loving, emotionally connected with the client, full of compassion (without sympathy) and skillfully responsive to the client in a way that is felt by the client as caring.

The Method

In Hakomi, we call this way of being Loving Presence. It means, first and foremost, that we see the client as a source of inspiration and nourishment. We are receiving the client as a gift, as a source of nourishment for us. A radical idea! This receptive and appreciative state is not only nourishing for us as therapists, but is also felt by the client as a powerful reminder of their own personal strength and beauty and wholeness.

As Hakomi practitioners, we see ourselves, not as professional *experts* who will heal the client, but as skillful spiritual friends who accompany clients on their healing journey. The quality of relationship that this state of mind creates is tangible both to the client and to any observers. It is the evolved expression of the Hakomi principles of unity, organicity, mindfulness, wholeness and non-violence. The method now looks less and less mechanical, more and more like humans relating to humans. The practitioner is relating to the client as one person with another. This is the key to most missing experiences for most people - this kind and loving way of being witnessed and related to.

So the four key characteristics of the Hakomi way are:
1. the practice of loving presence and all that entails,
2. a constant focus on present experience (both the what and the how, using nonverbal expression, emotion, memory, etc as sources of information about present experience and indicators of habits),
3. the use of little experiments in mindfulness for assisted self-study,
4. and a movement as soon as possible in the direction of the nourishing missing embodied experience.

The Nature
of Mind and Brain

From the Handbook 2010

States of Consciousness

The phrase "state of mind" or "state of consciousness" has much more precise meaning nowadays that it had just a few decades ago. Neurological research has revealed much more exactly what states the brain can be in when people interact. Many books have been written on the interaction of caregivers and the infants in their care. Adults in relationship also affect each others' state of mind. For the very intimate relationship between a therapist and client, the therapist's conscious awareness and deliberate control of his or her state of mind is essential. The effect of the therapist's state of mind on the process of this method is without doubt the single most important factor in its success. It should be noted that, in this aspect, the method is solidly aligned with the most universal spiritual teachings: agape in Christianity, compassion and mindfulness in Buddhism, nonviolence and non-separation in both.

Ron lists possible states of consciousness of the therapist :
- ordinary conversational way of being with someone – this is just the way people talk normally.
- loving presence, a state of both presence and compassion.
- empathetic. *"We can't feel anything that happens outside ourselves, but by unconsciously merging self and other, the other's experiences echo within us. We feel them as if they're our own."* (de Waal, 2009)
- silence, a state in which we are waiting, relaxed and quiet, offering space when the client needs it. In his final years of teaching, he, (Ron Kurtz) taught his students "the judicious use of silence."
- observing-searching, an habitual awareness of nonverbal aspects of the client's behavior. In Hakomi this is called 'tracking'.

- modelling-designing, the ability to think and plan, to get ideas about the client's history and beliefs from the observation of indicators and the creation of experiments based on those observations
- comforting. *"Comforting body contact is part of our mammalian biology, going back to maternal nursing, holding, and carrying which is why we both seek and give it under stressful circumstances. People touch and hug at funerals, in hospitals around sick or injured loved ones, during wars and earthquakes and following defeat in sports."* (de Waal, 2009)

Ron also lists states of consciousness that a client might be experiencing and to which the therapist needs to be aware, attuned and skillful.
- conversational
- anxious or nervous which is common in first sessions or early in a session.
- mindful or hypnogogic. This state has a quality of ready access to the unconscious mind, where the barriers between mind and body are relaxed. *"What the mind ponders, the body enacts. What the body experiences, the mind absorbs."* (Ford, 1989)
- emotional but non-traumatic.
- traumatic (hijacked). This is a special state in which a reliving of an overwhelming state of fear takes over the body and mind. (See Levine or Ogden)
- childlike, experiencing oneself as the child one once was, usually in a vividly remembered situation.
- healing state where a spontaneous sequence of events returns one to wholeness through emotion, insight and integration, controlled primarily by the adaptive unconscious.

> The next few sections include quotes and Ron's commentary on them

Consciousness as Choice

Some quotes on consciousness as choice:

> *"You can't do what you want, till you know what you're doing."*
> *(Feldenkrais as cited in Kaetz, 2007)*

> *"Sensations that are qualia-laden afford the luxury of choice. So now we have identified two functional features of qualia: irrevocability on the input side and flexibility on the output side. ... There is a third important feature of qualia. In order to make decisions on the basis of qualia-laden representation, the representation needs to exist long enough for you to work with it."*
> *(Ramachandran, 1988)*

> *"Just as intelligence has been described as 'What you use when you don't know what to do,' when no standard response will suffice, so too consciousness is prominently involved when the situation contains ambiguity or demands creative responses, ones that cannot be handled by a decision tree. Many mental activities can be handled by subroutines; consciousness helps to deal with the leftovers (and create new subroutines for the next time)." (Calvin, 1998)*

The Nature of Mind and Brain

Ron's comments on the quotes:

It's not just mental activities that can be handled by subroutines; lots of physical acts can also be subroutines. Some are inherited, like swallowing. These are called fixed action patterns. They form more complex structures called general action patterns.

Subroutines, mental or physical, or mental-physical combinations, form more complex routines. So, at every level, remembering Ken Wilber (1995), anything is both a part of a larger whole and a whole made up of smaller parts. It's parts and wholes all the way down. It's also routines and subroutines all the way down the living ladder. Every operation is a subroutine of larger operations and a routine made of smaller subroutines.

When a mental activity is "handled by subroutines", it's more than likely done without conscious attention, outside of consciousness. Bargh and Chartrand (1999) use the word non-conscious. In their paper "The Unbearable Automaticity of Being" they describe several experiments on automatic behaviors. A whole book devoted to this subject is Strangers to Ourselves by Timothy D. Wilson (2002)

Consciousness is Limited

> *"Consciousness is limited because the nervous system's overall mode of operation... attempts at all times to increase its computational efficiency while lowering its computational overhead."... (Llinás, 2002)*

Consciousness can only handle so much load or information processing. This concept is discussed by Sweller as the Cognitive Load Theory (2003). Consciousness is subject to ego depletion. And, as we saw above in the quote from Ramachandran (1998), consciousness needs time, because alternatives are being considered.

Our general goal is to make certain things conscious that were unconscious, to consider alternatives where there were only automatic subroutines.

> *"You can't be conscious of what you're not conscious of." (Jaynes, 1976)*

That's where mindfulness comes in.

Becoming Conscious of What?

> *"What do you get when you fall in love?*
> *You get another chance to catch pneumonia.*
> *And when you do,*
> *He'll never phone ya'*
> *I'll never fall in love again.*
> *I'll never fall in love again"*
> *(Hal David, 1968)*

How's that for "construing the situation"? You have to figure someone believing that mental concept could be harboring an unconscious memory of a painful experience of falling in love and that the experience was never integrated and resolved. The experience never lost its influence on the person. The adaptive unconscious has become organized to "never fall in love again". Without deliberate effort or some corrective positive experience to counter it, the long forgotten experience remains influential and as Pierre Janet (1921) puts it, "an irritation".

It was Janet's theory that certain experiences overwhelm a person's ability to synthesize reality into a meaningful whole.

> *"During these periods of abaissement, Janet found, our psyche seems to lose some of its capacity to synthesize reality into a meaningful whole. If we encounter a traumatic or strong emotional event during these periods, the mind lacks its usual ability to make sense of it and fit it properly into a meaningful, secure whole (as cited in Ellenberger, 1970, and Rossi & Smith, 1990). During abaissement, we tend to be emotionally vulnerable and easily overwhelmed; we can register the life experiences, but we cannot properly 'digest' them. The emotional experience floats in our unconscious, unassimilated, in effect, jamming the gears of the mind. Janet hypothesized that such unassimilated experiences could become the seed of psychological or psychosomatic illness, obsessive thought*

patterns, phobias—all sorts of behavioral problems. Many chronic problems, he believed, were the result of the mind-body's continuing, frustrated effort to make sense of the original disturbing experience.

Janet believed that there was an underlying physiological source of the abaissements during the day that was somehow associated with stress and exhaustion. One medical historian of this era summarized Janet's view: "We do not know the exact nature of psychological forces." Janet never doubted that they were of a physiological nature, and seems to have believed that the day would come when they could be measured. He considered that these forces were, to a great extent, connected with the condition of the brain and organs... and differ from one individual to another. These forces can be reconstituted in some way. "I don't know what these reserves are, but I do know that they exist," said Janet. One of the main sources of this reconstitution is sleep; hence the importance for the therapist to teach his client about the best way of preparing himself for sleep. The same could be said about the various techniques of rest and relaxation, the distribution of pauses throughout the day, of rest days during the month, and of vacations during the year..." (as cited in Ellenberger, 1970)

A strong emotional event that remains unassimilated requires some very specific support to finally become assimilated and the individual returned to normal functioning. First of all, the event must be returned to consciousness. The initial procedures of the Hakomi method—the client's commitment, mindfulness, experiments—are designed for this. Once the event and its associated feelings have been activated, the procedures focus on integrating it, which means facing it, making sense of it and assimilating it.

Often an important element of an emotional event that is being assimilated is the presence of a sympathetic, caring person who supports the individual through the pain and confusion of the event; for a child, that's usually a parent, a caretaker or an older sibling, and for the client, it's the therapist or, when I work, it can be my assistants.

When you hold a client during the time of emotional expression and integration, you could be supplying exactly what was missing during the original event. Maybe the people who were there were causing the problem and the pain. Or they were too disturbed themselves to be able to offer what was needed. Maybe no one was there to offer comfort or—as Al Pesso once told me— simply to bear witness. It always needs someone to be there. When someone [like a small child] doesn't have the "capacity to synthesize reality into a meaningful whole", it needs someone to help, a calm, sympathetic, patient and understanding person, someone to care for a soul in pain. When a client is reliving an old painful event, your silent presence and your kindness can provide the support needed for healing.

It has been argued before that some experiences remain "unfinished" and that completing them has therapeutic value. Fritz Perls called them "unfinished business". The idea has been out there for a while. The method of self-discovery is a process that works with such experiences to complete them.

I'll try in this short paper to give a very general description of that process. But first, two other ideas that are important to our discussion.

> *"Psychotherapy, like other forms of medical intervention, is now expected to be "evidence-based," and the evidence doesn't support the view that talking about childhood experiences has therapeutic value. Research shows that the effective forms of psychotherapy are those that focus on people's current problems, rather than their ancient history." (Rich Harris, 2006)*

I'll try reconciling these two points of view, the idea of undigested childhood experiences and the research evidence that talking about childhood doesn't help. But first I would like to introduce one of my own ideas about missing experiences. I propose that when painful experiences don't complete, it is because something very general was missing, namely, the support for its completion. One of my questions is, what are those conditions and actions that support the completion of painful experiences. Here's what I think are the main supports: safety, time, the presence of a skilled, compassionate person, and the physical comfort needed to contain the whole completion process.

Safety is needed to allow the overwhelmed mind to turn inward and work on completing the experience. That process is called integration. Time is needed because integration takes time. What we do in Hakomi is start the process of integration in such a way that it has the strong possibility of completing; we don't always complete long-standing unintegrated experiences in one shot. Still, it may only need one good therapy session to start a process that leads naturally to a successful completion.

A skilled, compassionate person is needed because the initial effort to complete includes the effort to bring the unintegrated experience into present awareness and to contain the emotions released by that awareness. The Hakomi Method is exactly how this is done.

The Unconscious: Self-States

First, an excerpt

> *"One can ... compare the mind of a man to a theater of indefinite depth whose apron is very narrow but whose stage becomes larger away from the apron. On this lighted apron there is room for one actor only. He enters, gestures for a moment, and leaves; another arrives, then another, and so on.... Among the scenery and on the far-off backstage there are multitudes of obscure forms whom a summons can bring onto the stage... and unknown evolutions take place incessantly among this crowd of actors."*
>
> *(Taine, 1871)*

    The analogy here is between actors who can only appear one at a time and various self- states of which there are many but that also appear only one at time. Much is going on among the self-states "backstage" which is out of one's awareness. Keeping actors backstage is, in Bromberg's terms (2006), a function of "normal dissociation." In cases of trauma, dissociation is not the same; it results in loss of function.

    Either client or therapist or both may switch states and such switching will change the interpersonal relationship. The transition between self-states or states of mind is therefore a significant occurrence in the therapeutic relationship and is worthy of attention and discussion within a session where it occurs.

    One can compare the concept of self-states to unified adaptive patterns, each based on and evoked within a perceived context or situation, without conscious attention to the "switches" that occur between changing patterns. Psychology has proposed any number of sets of *sub-personalities*. What's common is the concept of the multiplicity of selves; however, in most theories, the sub-selves are in conflict. According to Phillip Bromberg (1998), they are just normally dissociated, so we can play our different roles without confusion. The gap between "actors" or self-states that switch from off-stage to on-stage is written about in "Standing in the Spaces".

As therapists we see these switches and gaps when clients enter emotional states; for example, following an experiment. We also see actors in conflict when a nourishing statement, offered during an experiment, is rejected. We can assume, in such cases, that there is an adaptive pattern that precludes accepting that kind of nourishment. We can also assume that this adaptive pattern evolved for purposes of affective protection in a situation that required such measures at the time.

Here's Bromberg's idea about trauma:

> "Psychological trauma can be looked at in different ways. I see it is as the precipitous disruption of self-continuity through the invalidation of the patterns of meaning that define the experience of 'who one is.' " (Bromberg, 1998)

Noticing transitions is another way of following a client's process. This is especially important when working with the outcome of an experiment. A change of "actors" (self-states) in the client may evoke a corresponding change in the therapist. For example, when a strong emotion arises in the client, compassion may arise in the therapist. When sadness arises, it can be responded to with a hand on the shoulder. A shift in the client to a child state should also be responded to by becoming gentle and using words a child would understand. Emotions and the child state are just a few self-states among many. In the process, we respond to shifts by contacting the client's new present experience. Bromberg, who practices a relational method, might respond with his own experience; for example, "I can see how sad you've become and I feel some sadness myself, just seeing it." Not a bad approach, I think.

Practicing attention to shifting self-states may lead to good guesses about the deeper organizing principles that influence the shifting. For example, the sense that a session is ending or the therapist is getting bored could prompt a client to ask one question after another or to become highly emotional or demonstrative in some other way. The organizing principle might be: keep people engaged at all costs.

The Amazing Case for How Unconscious We Are

Hakomi deals with the organization of experience. For people having experiences — that's you, me and everyone else — an experience just happens, full blown and immediate. We see what we see without feeling or sensing how the brain creates images. We see the shapes and colors, we speak words and sentences, we make hundreds of movements with our eyes, all without experiencing how our brains do these things. All experience is the outcome of complex organizing processes of the brain, processes that take place outside of consciousness.

1. From *Who's Minding the Mind (Carey, 2007)*

    "The new studies reveal a subconscious brain that is far more active, purposeful and independent than previously known. Goals, whether to eat, mate or devour an iced latte, are like neural software programs that can only be run one at a time, and the unconscious is perfectly capable of running the program it chooses.

    We're finding that we have these unconscious behavioral guidance systems that are continually furnishing suggestions through the day about what to do next, and the brain is considering and often acting on those, all before conscious awareness." Dr. Bargh added: *"Sometimes those goals are in line with our conscious intentions and purposes, and sometimes they're not." "Sometimes non-conscious effects can be bigger in sheer magnitude than conscious ones,"* Dr. Schaller said, *"because we can't moderate stuff we don't have conscious access to, and the goal stays active." The brain appears to use the very same neural circuits to execute an unconscious act as it does a conscious one."*

2. From *Strangers to Ourselves (Wilson, 2004)*

> "...the modern view of the adaptive unconscious is that a lot of the interesting stuff about the human mind— judgments, feelings, motives—occur outside of awareness for reasons of efficiency, and not because of repression. Just as the architecture of the mind prevents low-level processing (e.g. perceptual processes) from reaching consciousness, so are many higher-order psychological processes and states inaccessible."

3. From *Making Up The Mind: How the Brain Creates our Mental World (Frith, 2007)*

> "We do not perceive the object in front of our eyes until the brain has made unconscious inferences about what that object may be. We are not aware of the action we are about to perform until the brain has made an unconscious choice about what that action should be."

4. From *The Itch (Gawande, 2008)*

> "Such findings open up a fascinating prospect: perhaps many patients whom doctors treat as having a nerve injury or a disease have, instead, what might be called sensor syndromes. When your car's dashboard warning light keeps telling you that there is an engine failure, but the mechanics can't find anything wrong, the sensor itself may be the problem. This is no less true for human beings. Our sensations of pain, itch, nausea, and fatigue are normally protective. Unmoored from physical reality, however, they can become a nightmare."

5. From *The Unbearable Automaticity of Being (Bargh & Chartrand, 1999)*

> *"....none put it so vividly as the philosopher A. N. Whitehead: "It is a profoundly erroneous truism, repeated by all copy-books and by eminent people making speeches, that we should cultivate the habit of thinking of what we are doing. The precise opposite is the case. Civilization advances by extending the number of operations which we can perform without thinking about them. Operations of thought are like cavalry charges in a battle – they are strictly limited in number, they require fresh horses, and must only be made at decisive moments."*

6. From *I of the vortex (Llinas, 2002)*

> *"...the nervous system's overall mode of operation...attempts at all times to increase its computational efficiency while lowering its computational overhead.... Comforting or disturbing, the fact is that we are basically dreaming machines that construct virtual models of the real world. It is probably as much as we can do with only one and a half pounds of mass and a 'dim' power consumption of 14 watts."*

7. From *Looking for Spinoza: Joy, Sorrow, and the Feeling Brain (Damasio, 2003)*

> *"All living organisms from the humble amoeba to the human are born with devices designed to solve automatically, no proper reasoning required, the basic problems of life."*

Commentary on the Previous References:

In *Who's Minding the Mind* (2007), Carey states: *"[a subconscious brain is] more active, purposeful and independent than previously known."* Quoting Dr. Mark Schaller, a psychologist at the University of British Columbia, *"Sometimes non conscious effects can be bigger in sheer magnitude than conscious ones because we can't moderate stuff we don't have conscious access to, and the goal stays active."* The stuff lasts and lasts. The adaptive unconscious is active and normally inaccessible. Wilson also says this in *Strangers To Ourselves (2002)*. Of course, many spiritual practices and methods of psychotherapy are attempting to overcome this all too normal state of affairs and to access the adaptive unconscious. The differences lie in the way the various methods do this. In Hakomi, we do it by creating and implementing brief, concise experiments while the client is in a mindful state.

In *Strangers to Ourselves (2002)*, Wilson tells us that *"judgments, feelings, motives—occur outside of awareness for reasons of efficiency, and not because of repression."* Repression does occur, but it's not the primary function of the unconscious. The primary function of the adaptive unconscious is to conserve consciousness, to save it for things that need prolonged concentration and deliberation, situations for which there are no habitual reactions. When we attempt to bring the activity of the adaptive unconscious into consciousness, we do it by noticing habitual behaviors and by working to help the client notice them.

In *Making Up The Mind (2007)*, Frith is one of the pioneers of neural imaging. He studied the activity of the brain as decisions were being made. He discovered that what we do is not usually decided by conscious deliberation; the brain begins to implement most behaviors before we are conscious of this happening. The moment to moment activity that is our daily life, which we may believe we are responsible for, is carried out by subconscious actors whose motives and history we may not have access to. Think, if you will, of all those habits that are hard to break! When was the last time that you had the thought, "I think I'll bite my nails now."

In *The Itch (2008)*, Gawande gives us the term, *"sensor syndrome"*. Our sensations, he says, can become, *"Unmoored from physical reality."* It's not just our ideas that can be "unmoored", our sensations can! Our experiences themselves. When this happens, they appear totally real to us, but are in fact, only a kind of dreaming of the brain.

As Llinás writes in *I of the vortex (2002)*, *"the brain is a virtual reality machine"*.... *"Consider that the waking state is a dreamlike state (in the same sense that dreaming is a wakelike state)"*.

In *Looking for Spinoza (2003)*, Damasio names the automaticity of life itself, *"from the humble amoeba to the human"*.

Of course it had to be this way. The process of evolution solved "the basic problems of life" billions of years before consciousness arose. Think of flowers turning towards the sun! Biological, chemical solutions, like DNA, that work without thought, used over and over again for billions of years. Evolution is a keeper of what works. When it solves a problem, the solution is used repeatedly in variations and new species. We may expect that even consciousness has been used before, but no doubt only in the very limited way we are able to use it.

The Nature of Mind and Brain

> Excerpts from Timothy Wilson's book *Strangers to Ourselves (2004)* and commentary from Ron Kurtz regarding the application of Wilson's ideas to the Hakomi Method.

The Adaptive Unconscious

"All men have two reasons for everything they do: a good reason and the real reason." —Anonymous

"A picture has emerged of a set of pervasive, adaptive, sophisticated mental processes that occur largely out of view. Indeed, some researchers have gone so far as to suggest that the unconscious mind does virtually all the work and that conscious will may be an illusion."
(Wilson, 2004)

Wilson's book brings light to the fact that we are much less aware or consciously in control than we ordinarily assume. What's new here is that the unconscious, the adaptive unconscious, is not the Freudian unconscious with its repressive forces and powerful, irrational impulses. Wilson states that

> "...the modern view of the adaptive unconscious is that a lot of the interesting stuff about the human mind—judgments, feelings, motives—occur outside of awareness for reasons of efficiency, and not because of repression. Just as the architecture of the mind prevents low-level processing (e.g. perceptual processes) from reaching consciousness, so are many higher-order psychological processes and states inaccessible." (Wilson, 2002)

Wilson's book is concerned with two main questions: Why is it that people often do not know themselves very well (e.g., their own characters, why they feel the way they do, or even the feelings themselves)? And how can they increase their self-knowledge?

Since Hakomi is a method for gaining self-knowledge, these two questions that Wilson raises are totally relevant to our work. The heart of our work, like much psychodynamic psychotherapy, is exactly this: making unconscious mental processes conscious. We do other things also, but the core of the work is just that.

The description of the adaptive unconscious noted above: *"pervasive, adaptive, sophisticated mental processes that occur largely out of view" (Wilson, 2004)*, points to a significant difference between this recent view and the earlier, psychoanalytic view. I believe this is a very different image of the unconscious than earlier images. Although this first began to change with Jung's realization of the vast and positive aspects of the unconscious, it is only now being realized as the pervasive, automatic moulder of action and experience that it truly is. We are only now beginning to grasp what the contemplative and meditative traditions have always known: we are largely automatic and unaware. For example, in his bestseller book *Blink* (2005) Gladwell discusses both Wilson and Bargh. It has always been known in those spiritual disciplines where meditation and mindfulness are central practices. Without such practice, the truth of our automaticity is difficult to realize.

Here's how one spiritual teacher describes the realization:

> *"Somewhere in this process (meditation), you will come face to face with the sudden and shocking realization that you are completely crazy. Your mind is a shrieking, gibbering madhouse on wheels barreling pell-mell down the hill, utterly out of control and hopeless. No problem. You are not crazier that you were yesterday. It has always been this way, and you just never noticed. You are also not crazier than anybody else around you. The real*

difference is that you have confronted the situation; they have not. So they still feel relatively comfortable. That does not mean that they are better off. Ignorance may be bliss, but it does not lead to Liberation. So, don't let this realization unsettle you. It is a milestone actually, a sign of real progress. The very fact that you have looked at the problem straight in the eye means that you are on your way up and out of it." (Gunaratana, 2011)

"Nor is the unconscious a single entity with a mind and will of its own. Rather, humans possess a collection of modules that have evolved over time and operate outside of consciousness." (Wilson, 2002)

For me (Kurtz), this is the second big realization. We are "modular." One simple example is the visual system. It has over fifty separate neural circuits, each one having a particular part in creating what appears in consciousness as a unified, integrated, stable visual image. The amount of processing that's needed to create that image is prodigious and enormously complex. Yet, we are normally aware of nothing but the outcome.

Another example is seen in those theories of personality that talk about sub-selves, sub-personalities or "parts." (Schwarz, 1995). Several books examine what certain neurological disorders reveal about the brain and nervous system's modularity. Two of these are *Phantoms in the Brain* by V. S. Ramachandran (1998) and *Altered Egos: How the Brain Creates the Self* by Todd E. Feinberg (2001).

Automaticity is necessary and that's why so much goes on outside of consciousness.

"Consciousness is a limited capacity system, and to survive in the world, people must be able to process a great deal of information outside of awareness.

The Nature of Mind and Brain

> *... a lot of the interesting stuff about the human mind — judgments, feelings, motives — occur outside of awareness for reasons of efficiency, and not because of repression."* (Wilson, 2002)

Un-consciousness is the result of our need to conserve consciousness. Wilson also states that *"many higher-order psychological processes and states [are] inaccessible."* Of course that's true and the visual system is a good example. But for our purpose, which is to bring unconscious material into consciousness, we have to be more precise about what is accessible and what is not. When we evoke a reaction by doing an experiment with the client in mindfulness, the outcome is usually a reaction that the client notices. The reaction is neither deliberate nor intentional. When it is noticed, it is an instance of the automatic being observed. Still, it has a purpose. It is an action taken by the adaptive unconscious. It is adaptation in action. And it may very well be an adaptation to a much earlier life situation, a situation with little or no current reality.

If an emotion is experienced, it could be one that was active though the client was not aware of it.

We can then say that we have accessed the adaptive unconscious or at least, we have observed its activity (see Damasio, 2003). If the reaction is a thought or a memory that was shaping the client's experience without the client being aware that it was doing so, then again, we have accessed the adaptive unconscious. We often evoke long buried memories and surprising thoughts, which have been active outside of consciousness and shaping both actions and experiences. The client's history often bears this out. In this way, we are accessing the adaptive unconscious. Some of what we access is immediate and temporary. Some is the more pervasive mental structures and habits that have shaped whole lifetimes. I think Wilson could be convinced of this, if he witnessed the work we do. The power of this work is just this: it accesses quickly and precisely.

> *"Repression may not, however, be the most important reason why people do not have conscious access to thoughts, feelings, or motives. The implications of this fact for how to gain access to the unconscious cannot be underestimated and are a major topic of this book."* (Wilson, 2004))

The unconscious is not in business just to repress (although it can and will sometimes do that!) A result is this: it should be much easier to access the unconscious than repression theory implies. If the main reason for an adaptive unconscious is the conservation of consciousness, then with the proper conditions—like the inner, passive focus of mindfulness—it should be relatively easy to access core material. That's exactly what we find.

> *"... a good deal of human perception, memory, and action occurs without conscious deliberation or will..."* (Wilson, 2004)

Deliberation, according to Ramachandran (1998), is making a choice from a set of options and it is the main function of consciousness.

> *"People develop habitual "tendencies of thought" that are nonconscious."* (Wilson, 2004)

I call these implicit beliefs. They are important components of core material.

> *" The adaptive unconscious is thus more than just a gatekeeper, deciding what information to admit to consciousness. It is also a spin doctor that interprets information outside of awareness. ...events in the environment can trigger goals and direct our behavior completely outside of*

The Nature of Mind and Brain

> *consciousness....The adaptive unconscious thus plays a major executive role in our mental lives."*
> *(Wilson, 2004)*

The adaptive unconscious directs. It's a major executive. It's active and can be quite independent of conscious intent. Think of alien hand syndrome.

> *"Our unconscious minds develop chronic ways of interpreting information from our environments."*
> *(Wilson, 2004)*

We jump first and think "Snake" after. Almost immediately after, we realize, "Oh, it's only a piece of rope." But we've already jumped and had a surge of fear. We didn't stop and think at all. It all happened without conscious deliberation or decision. So, who said it was a snake? The adaptive unconscious did. Did it know it was a snake? No! It couldn't have; it wasn't a snake. It interpreted the image perceived as a snake and it immediately decided to jump out of the way. It did it without conscious awareness that the interpretation or the decision was being made. The jumper becomes aware mid-jump perhaps or even later.

Still, in most cases, it's better to think a rope is a snake than to think a snake is a rope. Of course there's no thinking at all if the adaptive unconscious is handling it and that's the point. You think you're just going for your evening walk and you surprise yourself by ending up at your old girlfriend's house. Blaise Pascal put it poetically this way, *"The heart has reasons that reason knows not of."* Or you are having a long, internal conversation with someone you're really angry with... while you're driving to work. Who's paying attention to traffic lights and the cars around you? Who was driving? It's not that conscious, deliberate person you think of as yourself. By now, I'm sure you know. It's your driving habits, good or bad.

Core material such as emotions, memories, and implicit beliefs, is certainly influential in un- conscious interpretations. One simple way to work with interpretations is to offer a statement while the client is in mindfulness and ask the client to notice how he or she interprets what you're saying. "What do I seem to be saying when I tell you..." and then offer the statement.

> *"People's judgments and interpretations are often guided by a quite different concern, namely the desire to view the world in the way that gives them the most pleasure—what might be called the "feel-good" criterion. ... people go to great lengths to view the world in a way that maintains a sense of well-being. ... When it comes to maintaining a sense of well-being, each of us is the ultimate spin doctor."*
> *(Wilson, 2004)*

In Dietrich Dörner's prize winning book, *The Logic of Failure* (2007), he describes research showing that one important reason people fail to solve complex problems is the strong tendency to maintain a sense of competence. Because of this tendency to protect and provide a sense of well being, much of what causes unnecessary suffering is, paradoxically, motivated to do the opposite. In working with "parts" or sub-selves, we can assume they are all acting in what they believe is the best interest of the client. The behavior of these parts implies certain beliefs (just like the jumping away implied a belief about a snake). An example that comes up in therapy would be a person reacting with disbelief when someone offers love. The reaction is protection against possible hurt, should that love be false or be lost. And the implicit belief is: accepting love is dangerous for that reason, it could result in hurt. And you can bet there's a memory or two of that exact thing happening.

> *"What makes us feel good depends on our culture and our personalities and our level of self-esteem, but the desire to feel good, and the ability to meet this desire with non conscious thought, are probably universal....*
> *...Before considering how best to obtain self-knowledge, we need to make at least some headway on such questions as whether it makes any difference to know ourselves. Does gaining insight (becoming conscious of previously*

unknown things about ourselves) change anything? Does the person who has limited insight into the reasons for her actions, for example, behave any differently from the person who has great insight?" (Wilson, 2004)

Of course insight makes a difference. People change. They change what they can experience and they change the meanings they give to events. These changes, when acted upon with success become the new operations of the adaptive unconscious. These are the changes we work to initiate and reinforce.

> *"Perhaps the best use of consciousness is to put ourselves in situations in which our adaptive unconscious can work smoothly. This is best achieved by recognizing what our non-conscious needs and traits are and planning accordingly."*
> (Wilson, 2004)

This seems to be part of a new movement in psychology, called "positive psychology." Martin Seligman has written a book called *Authentic Happiness* (2002). His thesis is that we have certain signature strengths and limited ranges of what we can be. Happiness is using our strengths and "dealing with" our limitations. Other books that speak to this are Bruce Lipton's *The Biology of Belief* (2005) and *Genuine Happiness: Meditation as the Path to Fulfillment* by B. Alan Wallace and His Holiness the Dalai Lama (2005).

> *"Automatic thinking has five defining features: it is non conscious, fast, unintentional, uncontrollable, and effortless.... we can define automaticity as thinking that satisfies all or most of these criteria."*
> (Wilson, 2004)

Good to remember these five features. When we watch to see if clients are reacting and when we listen to them reporting their reactions, these five features can be kept in mind.

- Non conscious. Often we can see physical signs of reactions that the client doesn't notice.
- Fast. We're looking for what happens immediately. We say when we're doing an experiment, "Please tell me your immediate reaction when..."
- Unintentional. Clients are often surprised at their reactions. That's a good sign.
- Uncontrollable. Painful emotions can arise spontaneously and repeating an experiment often results in the exact same reaction.
- Effortless. Effort is more likely to be expended trying to control the reaction after it's started happening. These reactions do not carry the experience of what can be called conscious will.

> *"...Once a correlation is learned, the non-conscious system tends to see it where it does not exist, thereby becoming more convinced that the correlation is true"...."The non-conscious mind can jump to conclusions quite quickly."*
> *(Wilson, 2004)*

The adaptive unconscious is built for speed, the kind that works in the jungle (where the snakes aren't ropes) and saves your butt.

> *"Mischel argued, personality is better conceived as a set of unique cognitive and affective variables that determine how people construe the situation. People have chronic ways of interpreting and evaluating different situations, and it is these interpretations that influence their behavior."*
> *(as cited in Wilson, 2004)*

I now prefer this way of thinking about people. I don't use character typing very much anymore. I find observing present behavior and guessing about implicit beliefs from those observations more varied, precise and useful. I think Mischel (1968) is right: this is actually how personality works in the real world. A good book to read is *Why They Kill* by Richard Rhodes (1999). They kill, he says, because they interpret the situation as calling for killing. They were taught to interpret certain situations that way. My central thesis is that human personality resides in two places: in the adaptive unconscious and in the conscious construals of the self. The adaptive unconscious meets Allport's (1954) definition of personality: "The dynamic organization within the individual of those psychophysical systems that determine his characteristic behavior and thought". It has distinctive, characteristic ways of interpreting the social environment and stable motives that guide people's behavior. ... These dispositions and motives are measurable with indirect techniques rather than by self-report questionnaires.

> *"But the conscious self also meets Allport's definition. Because people have no direct access to their non-conscious dispositions and motives, they must construct a conscious self from other sources. The constructed self consists of life stories, possible selves, explicit motives, self-theories, and beliefs about one's feelings and behaviors. Oddly, these two selves appear to be relatively independent. There is increasing evidence that people's constructed self bears little correspondence to the non-conscious self."* (Wilson, 2004)

First, you can see why questions aren't the way to get to the unconscious. Ask a question, you're going to get a construed" answer. You want to use experiments—which are just a better way to ask questions— if you want to talk to the adaptive unconscious. Second, there are two kinds of selves, conscious and non-conscious. In this work, we intentionally communicate with the adaptive unconscious, by our tone of voice and by contacting the experiences and actions that are controlled by it.

The Nature of Mind and Brain

The Nature of Belief

1. The brain is a virtual reality machine.

"Consider that the waking state is a dreamlike state (in the same sense that dreaming is a wake like state) guided and shaped by the senses, whereas regular dreaming does not involve the senses at all. Although the brain may use the senses to take in the richness of the world, it is not limited by those senses; it is capable of doing what it does without any sensory input whatsoever. The nature of the brain and what it does makes the nervous system a very different type of entity from the rest of the universe. It is, as stated repeatedly, a reality emulator...

...Comforting or disturbing, the fact is that we are basically dreaming machines that construct virtual models of the real world. It is probably as much as we can do with only one and a half pounds of mass and a "dim" power consumption of 14 watts."
(Llinás, 2002)

2. Experiments with Hypnosis

Ernst Hilgard did many experiments on hypnosis, one of which was with a blind person. Hilgard induced hypnotic deafness in the man and proceeded to test its effectiveness by making sudden loud noises. He also observed and measured the man's reactions. With all of these stimuli, there were no noticeable reactions.

As a second part of the experiment, Hilgard said to the same hypnotized subject, "Perhaps there is some part of you that is hearing my voice and processing the information. If there is, I should like the index finger of your right hand to rise as a sign that this is the case" (Hilgard, 1977, p. 186). The right index finger immediately went up. When awakened from the hypnotized state, Hilgard asked the subject if anything unusual happened. The man replied that the only thing he noticed was that at one point, his index finger arose unexpectedly and on its own. Hilgard theorized that this indicated that there existed a hidden observer, operating outside of consciousness. This is credible evidence for the reality of the adaptive unconscious.

3. The Socialization System as per Judith Rich Harris

The three personality systems, according to Harris, are the developmental, socialization, and status systems. She shows, using research, how personality (which for us means the habits and beliefs that run automatic behavior) is primarily the result of two factors, genetics and socialization (meaning primarily the influence of one's peer group). Many of the beliefs that run our behavior are culturally taught and supported by one's peers. I highly recommend her book *No Two Alike (2006)* and also Pinker's *The Blank Slate: The Modern Denial of Human Nature* (2002).

4. Implicit Reality: Implicit Beliefs in Action

"Implicit memory [sometimes called procedural memory, sometimes emotional memory] involves parts of the brain that do not require conscious processing during encoding or retrieval. When implicit memory is retrieved, the neural net profiles that are reactivated involve circuits in the brain that are a fundamental part of our everyday experience of life: behaviors, emotions, and images. These implicit elements form part of the foundation for our subjective sense of ourselves: we act, feel, and imagine without recognition of the influence of past experience on our present reality."   *(Siegel, 1999)*

I've noticed that the big moments in therapy are those in which the client realizes a significant belief about herself and her world that she didn't know she had. Such beliefs are often implicit, reflecting a reaction to some foundational experience. Such reactions develop into habits for dealing with all similar situations. Being implicit, the belief

The Nature of Mind and Brain

is not normally available to consciousness. In effect, it is an unchallenged idea about the nature of reality. I've talked about such beliefs as core beliefs, so habitual they are never questioned. They operate outside of consciousness. They make up the world we assume, without knowing we're assuming it. They are the frame of reference we long ago adopted in which we are still immersed. At best we have only the faintest inkling that we had anything to do with creating them.

The work of assisted self-discovery is to make these normally implicit beliefs and realities conscious. When the implicit beliefs are mistaken or highly negative—prompting negative thoughts and painful emotions—they inevitably cause suffering. Because the beliefs are mistaken, when the truth is more positive, the suffering is unnecessary. Being implicit, they are also difficult to realize, challenge or change. Such beliefs define who we are. For a Hakomi therapist, implicit beliefs have to be surmised from behavior, gestures, facial expressions and other signs of organization, signs that are called indicators.

We are dreaming machines and these beliefs are who we're dreaming ourselves to be. Clients, in the most important moments of their therapeutic work, discover who they're dreaming themselves to be and the world they've been dreaming they're living in. They are surprised to discover that these dreams can be revised. The work we do helps people change their implicit realities. Of course, once they're conscious, they're no longer implicit, and being conscious, they can be challenged and renegotiated. A person's reality, which in each unconscious moment seems the very ground he is standing on, turns out to be only a platform and not the true, good earth. Such discoveries set the mind spinning. Integration is the process whereby the spinning subsides and we're standing firmly on new ground.

So, we can ask about our clients, "What are your implicit realities? What worlds are you living in? And, who are you in those worlds?" Self discovery yields answers to those questions.

Implicit Beliefs and Rules

> *"Children learn a mental grammar by listening to a language (deaf children by observing sign language). They are acquisitive of associations as well as new words, and one fancy set of associations constitutes the mental grammar of a particular language. Starting at about eighteen months of age, children start to figure out the local rules and eventually begin using them in their own sentences. They may not be able to describe the parts of speech, or diagram a sentence, but their "language machine" seems to know all about such matters after a year's experience."* (Calvin, 2000)

An ordinary child develops habits of speech based on the patterns of the language spoken around and to him quite early in life. Later, the child may also learn, as facts, the names of the rules of grammar that describe those patterns. He may even think critically about them. When he does that, he's using a different part of his brain than the one he used to learn the patterns in the first place. Even if he doesn't learn the rules of grammar as facts and isn't able to think about them, he is still able to speak the language that uses them. He knows them implicitly. There are two very different kinds of learning, one where patterns are recognized and habits are developed without verbal thought or memory; and a second kind that thinks in words about things and remembers them as facts. Anyone who studies people and other animals, can hardly miss these differences.

Every infant also learns the patterns of relationships that she's embedded in. Without thinking about them in words, she learns to expect whatever it is that is consistently part of her world. She learns as best she can to deal with her world and her ways of dealing become the core habits that give her self and her life the shape it takes.

This shaping starts even before she's born. Conditions in the womb, the emotions of the mother who is carrying her, all these have an effect. Later in life, she may also learn to describe these things as facts, in words and sentences. If she makes the effort, maybe through meditation or by doing psychotherapy, she may also come to discover and consciously understand the implicit rules and convictions that organize who she is and what she can experience. Through this process of discovery and all the work it entails, she may be able to change in deep ways, ways that open her to a new, more nourishing world, a world that has been there all along but which her core patterns kept her from being a part of. If she doesn't discover the rules, chances are she won't change much.

I saw an old friend recently, after forty years of not being in touch. We're in our late sixties now. His way of relating hadn't changed at all. He was the same person I went to kindergarten and public school and high school with. It's not that I'd want him to be different; it's just that I could see how stable the "habit of who he is" had been.

The major task of experiential psychotherapy is the discovery of self. We work to help people become conscious of and understand the habits that control their experiencing. These habits can also be talked of as implicit rules. Bringing them into consciousness means that not only do we notice the actions and emotions they engender, we also learn to speak of them in words. We name them. We do this as part of changing them, changing the rules. When they change, people's experiences of themselves, others and the worlds they live in also change. That's what personal and spiritual growth are all about. There are other tasks that are part of the therapy, but discovery is the essential one.

A habit can be spoken of as implying a rule, and the rule could be described as a belief or a conviction. A habit of being friendly or seeking others, with all the feelings that go with that, could imply a rule like: "avoid being alone". The belief it implies might be: "closeness is pleasurable". It becomes a conviction when it is held firmly. For our purposes, that simply means it has strong emotions associated with it.

These habits, rules and convictions normally operate outside of consciousness. They act as organizing principles and motivating ideas. All of these terms—principles, rules, beliefs, convictions—convey a kind of awareness that isn't usually there. Deliberate, conscious thought is not there. These are all deep structures of the mind, learned through experiences, held in implicit memory. Like the rules of grammar they act quickly, without thought. Habits are necessary to both our sense of who we are and normal functioning. Reactions are needed in the real world, where time is of the essence and thinking can be a hindrance. Slipping on the ice is not a philosophical problem.

These deep structures of the mind are not explicit beliefs; they are "as if" beliefs. Since they have been learned through emotionally significant experiences, we can call them convictions. Beliefs may or may not have emotions associated with them. Convictions always have emotions associated with them. If we listen and look for the nonverbal expressions of convictions, we can use those expressions to evoke the emotions and the convictions associated with them. Observing people, we could say they are acting as if they had various convictions, though they may not be able to express some of them in words. The person's behavior, however, may suggest what those convictions are or even make them apparent to a skilled observer.

For example, some people hardly ever expect help. In most cases it's because they hold the conviction—again, without awareness—that other people will not help you, they expect you to be strong and do it yourself. In therapy, this conviction manifests itself when the client works without asking much from the therapist. The client thinks silently and makes very few comments on his or her experiences. It's as if the client does not expect the therapist to be interested or caring. Observing someone with this pattern, you could have a variety of hypotheses: he doesn't expect help, he believes he must do everything on his own, he's basically alone, others will always disappoint, it's not good to be beholden to others, it's weak to have needs, he's a burden to others. People have these kinds of convictions! It could be any of those or some combination. An experienced therapist can sense beliefs like these.

Most people have behavior patterns which are governed by rules they are not aware of, have not thought about and do not understand. An interested observer, however, might easily have ideas about the rules behind those patterns. In the example above, a therapist might notice certain behaviors: that the client considers things silently

The Nature of Mind and Brain

without engaging the therapist in the process, or the therapist might even begin to feel left out. A therapist trained to think about the nonverbal expressions of core material would quickly have ideas about self-reliance, weaknesses to be avoided, growing up too quickly and things like that.

Thinking about these 'as if' beliefs help therapists to understand clients' development, behaviors and how they organize their experiences. For example, a client might organize his needs into avoidance of any weaknesses. Understanding these things helps therapists make clients aware of them. In most people, these organizing influences are no more conscious than the organizing principles that govern riding a bicycle. Think of this: chimpanzees can learn to ride bicycles using the very same principles without ever having to talk about it.

We speak properly. We somehow know the how of grammar, without necessarily knowing the facts of grammar. Even though most of us cannot name all the rules of that grammar, we speak correctly. So, in some sense, we know the rules. But this knowing how is not the same as knowing facts. It's not the same kind of awareness. It's not in words. It's implicit. It's not thought, it's not conscious belief. Still, we're acting exactly as if we did believe. The beliefs are implicit.

We also relate to one another according to implicit rules. We relate as if we believed certain general things about people or ourselves. We have implicit beliefs about what kind of world it is and what kind of rules we should follow as people in that world. We follow these rules for relating, again, without being able to state them. They are not stored in our minds and brains as facts. They are part of the many things we learned through experiences and interactions throughout our lives. They are learned using the inherited, highly evolved method of pattern recognition. (see Siegel, 1999 and Lewis et al, 2001) This kind of learning and knowing are as old as life itself, infinitely older than words and thoughts. This is the knowing that runs our emotional and relational lives.

As body psychotherapists, we carefully observe clients' nonverbal expressions, postures, facial expressions, gestures, movement patterns, and general patterns of relating. We 'read' all that for what it says about the underlying rules, the experiences that created them and how they are still shaping present experience. We look for indicators of the client's core beliefs. Almost always, these 'as if' rules have been part of our lives since childhood. Since we learned them early, they also have the qualities of a child's beliefs: they are simple, over generalized and often inaccurate outside of what had been that child's immediate world. Being inaccurate and unavailable as ideas that can be examined, challenged and modified, they result in unnecessary suffering.

A part of a brain network, including the limbic system, holds the memories of this relational learning (see Panksepp, 2004 or Schore, 1994). This kind of memory is called implicit memory. Memories of the events in which this relational learning took place have strong emotions and images associated with them. For the person who has an implicit belief that "no one will help", the memories of being left alone to take care of herself are painful to recall. The need for others is kept from consciousness. A part of the brain makes sure of it. ("I'll never fall in love again!") In the Hakomi method, we've been calling these associated emotions, memories and images core material. When core material emerges into a client's consciousness, it usually appears first as a painful emotion or as a painful memory or visual image.

Implicit rules of relationship are learned early and they are simple rules. They have not been made complex by conceptual thinking. When they're made conscious, they can be stated in very simple sentences. Though adult behavior can be and in most cases is quite complex, the underlying rules are simple. They are rules like the one I've mentioned already: no one will help. Some others are: I'm not lovable. No one understands me. People will hurt me. I have to please everyone. There are many examples, but few are more complex than these.

Simple rules give rise to highly complex systems of behavior. This is one of the key discoveries of complexity theory (the repeated iteration of even a very simple formula can give rise to something as infinitely complex as the Mandelbrot Set). As Johnson (2001) points out, individual ants in a colony have only the simplest rules that operate locally and only govern each ant's reactions to the ants in its immediate surroundings. An individual ant knows nothing of the global behavior of the colony. As individuals, ants are not great thinkers – no one has ever succeeded in teaching an individual ant anything even as simple as a two choice maze. There are no boss ants. No one is in charge. No one is directing. The colony's "intelligence" and its highly complex behaviors emerge out of a few, simple, local rules. The colony responds successfully to continuously changing conditions. It almost seems to be conscious. By any reasonable criterion, it's intelligent. It's just not the conscious kind.

I have one, interesting example of the power of local rules. William R. Bartmann became a billionaire by changing one very simple local rule. Banks recover bad debts by paying people to pursue debtors and hound them with great persistence and much guilt slinging and accusatory language. On average, they get back 1% of their money. Bartmann became a billionaire by buying those same bad debts and recovered nine cents on the dollar on those same debts. He instituted one simple rule that all the people working for him as debt collectors followed: Be polite! This simple local rule earned him an 800% profit.

In the same way, the complexity of human relationships emerges out of the particular simple, local rules each of us learns in childhood. Many of these rules are cultural. A few are personal. For most people, the rules remain implicit, outside of awareness and govern without rational evaluation. So, as psychotherapists, we search for signs of something simple, something learned early and stored forever in the shadow world of implicit memory. Our most important and delicate task is to gently bring the light of consciousness to that shadowy world.

Mindfulness in Hakomi

"A change in the quality of attention, which passes from the looking-for to the letting-come."
(Depraz et al, 1999)

This combination of an open, vulnerable client and a therapist who is attempting to trigger reactions is exactly what makes the method work. Of course, clients know that this is the process. They understand what can happen. The procedure is voluntary and a completely cooperative effort. If the therapist is adroit enough, a client's reaction will be a source of insight—long buried feelings and memories will emerge. If the therapist is compassionate, then new experiences, of comfort, safety, hope and happiness, may become possible.

> In the next few sections Ron Kurtz writes about the inclusion of mindfulness in Hakomi. He gives some definitions as well as some practical pointers on how to use mindfulness in a session with a client in a Hakomi way.

The Client's Commitments: Mindfulness and Honesty

I give prospective clients a document that makes clear what will be expected of them. It says in part: This method is not about talking out your problems. There won't be long, speculative conversations about your troubles or your history. This method is designed to assist you in studying the processes that automatically create and maintain the person you have become. It is a method of assisted self-study. It requires that you enter into short periods of time where you become calm and centered enough to observe your own reactions, as if you were observing the behavior of another person, a state called mindfulness. The therapist assists your self-study by creating "little experiments" while you are in mindfulness. These experiments are always nonviolent and basically are designed to evoke reactions that will be reflections of the habits and beliefs that make you who you are. The implicit beliefs and relationship habits with which you meet the world automatically shape your present behavior. Aspects of your behavior, the aspects that reflect your deepest beliefs, are what the therapist uses to create the experiments.

The document goes on to say: The process works best: (1) if you can follow and report on your present experience; (2) if you're able to get into a calm inward focused state and are relaxed enough to allow reactions; (3) if you're willing to experience some painful feelings and speak about them; and (4) if you have the courage and be open and honest about your experience. That courage will be your greatest ally.

I have come to recognize that the method requires these four things of a client. Of course, some clients won't be able to do all this at first. There will have to be a "pre-study" phase in which other methods will have to be used. Such methods might be simply listening sympathetically without talking much, just indicating that you understand what the client is going through. It may take some time doing things like this to build the client's trust and to gain the cooperation of the client's adaptive unconscious, enough time to bring the client to the stage where he or she can enter mindfulness and allow reactions. I also tell clients about the rewards that are there for those who practice self-study.

> *"To study the Buddha Way is to study the self, to study the self is to forget the self, and to forget the self is to be enlightened by the ten thousand things." (Dogen, 1233)*

Of course the work we do is only a small step on that journey. And though the method is different, the attitude and direction are the same. Release from unnecessary suffering is release from an identity that includes habits and ideas that are not only old and outworn, but fundamentally flawed as descriptions of reality.

The Focus on Present Experience

Implicit Beliefs and Procedural Memory

> *"A picture has emerged of a set of pervasive, adaptive, sophisticated mental processes that occur largely out of view. Indeed, some researchers have gone so far as to suggest that the unconscious mind does virtually all the work and that conscious will may be an illusion."*
> *(Wilson, 2004)*

> *"Every creature with a brain has myriad predictions encoded in what it has learned."*
> *(Holland as cited in Waldrop, 1992)*

The one thing we most want to help clients discover and change is the habitual ways they create unnecessary suffering for themselves and others. The logic is this: Experience is organized by habits that function outside of consciousness. The most significant of these organizing habits are those that were learned early in life and developed in reaction to compelling, formative experiences (see Gerhardt, 2003; Schore 1994; Cassidy and Shave, Eds, 1999). Such habits are stored in implicit memory and are not normally accessible to consciousness. They are automated procedures, triggered by perceptions of internal and external realities, perceptions which themselves are influenced by organizing habits. Given all this, it's easy to see how the whole system can regress so easily into unsupported virtual realities. They are the functional equivalents of implicit beliefs.

These implicit predictions and beliefs exert a profound influence over everyday life without any simple, direct way to modify them. They influence all ongoing experience, whether it originates internally or externally, by producing the habitual reactions that result.

Mindfulness in Hakomi

They shape all manner of experience—perception, mood, thought, feeling and behavior. Thus, present experience is a reliable, immediate expression of non-conscious habits and beliefs. For that reason, we focus on present experiences and use them to bring what is normally unconscious into consciousness.

How the Mind Makes Meaning

"...this question of how much conscious control we have over our judgments, decisions, and behavior is one of the most basic and important questions of human existence." (Bargh and Chartrand, 1999)

When a statement offered to a person in a mindful state evokes a reaction that does not seem to be appropriate to the statement offered, more than likely it has been unconsciously translated. For example, when offered the statement, "I need more time to myself," the man's partner reacted by immediately feeling hurt. She was unconsciously translating the statement into, "You don't love me anymore." However, she was not conscious of doing that or even having that idea, only of feeling hurt.

This is typical when statements touch upon deeply held unconscious beliefs. These core beliefs act as "meaning attractors". Statements and events that are not even remotely similar can be automatically given meanings that reinforce the core belief. The reaction then is to the belief and not to what was actually said. The translations are unconscious processes that operate instantly between the moment of an event or a statement and the person's reaction to it.

When something like this happens in therapy, I ask the person to find the translation they're making. I say, "Notice what you hear when I say... or notice what meaning you are giving the statement you hear..." And then the original statement is offered again. Almost always, the person will notice the translation they're making.

It's not just statements that are unconsciously assigned meaning. All kinds of behaviors are also reacted to on the basis of how they've been unconsciously interpreted. Perceptions also are translated.

".... Perception is the brain's best guess about what is happening in the outside world. .... Our weaver-brain assembles as its best hypothesis of

> *what is out there from the slivers of information we get. Perception is inference."* (Gawande, 2008)

Gawande's article in the New Yorker Magazine is a real eye opener. Our belief that we are consciously creating our thoughts and behaviors is, as Nietzsche points out:

> *"The strongest knowledge–that of the total unfreedom of the human will–is nonetheless the poorest in successes, for it always has the strongest opponent: human vanity."* (Nietzsche, 1878)

To help people discover the sources of their habitual emotions and behaviors, to bring an understanding of automaticity and to have the techniques to bring habitual translators into consciousness are all extremely important and require great skill on the part of the Hakomi therapist.

History of Mindfulness Practice

"Mindfulness technologies have been applied in human endeavors for thousands of years. They have been found of great value by Hindus, Buddhists, Muslims, Christians; in India, Asia, Europe and America; in the far past, in the Middle Ages and in modern times. The depth and breadth of human experience with mindfulness technologies in itself argues very powerfully for their intrinsic worth in solving problems in inner experience, which is arguably the métier of clinical psychology." (Knight, 2009)

What Mindfulness is

Descriptions of Mindfulness from Ancient and Modern Sources:

"Sitting quietly and listening carefully to yourself, you can observe the main voice in which your thoughts recite themselves." (Thurman, 1999)

"According to the buddha dharma, spirituality means relating with the working basis of one's existence, which is one's state of mind. The method for beginning to relate directly with mind is the practice of mindfulness."
(Chögyam Trungpa, 2001)

"...the capacity to observe one's inner experience in what the ancient texts call a 'fully aware and non-clinging' way." (Schwartz and Begley, 2003)

> *"Bare Attention [mindfulness] is the clear and single-minded awareness of what actually happens to us and in us at the successive moments of perception."* (Nyanaponika Thera, 1972)

> *"The fundamental insight of most Eastern schools of spirituality, however, is that while thinking is a practical necessity, the failure to recognize thoughts as thoughts, moment after moment, is what gives each of us the feeling that we call "I," and this is the string upon which all our states of suffering and dissatisfaction are strung."*
> (Harris, 2004)

> *"Control of attention is the ultimate individual power."* (Brooks, 2008)

> *"Our ability to perceive the world around us seems so effortless that we tend to take it for granted. But just think of what's involved. You have two tiny upside down distorted images inside your eyeballs but what you see is a vivid three-dimensional world out there in front of you and this transformation is nothing short of a miracle."*
> (Ramachandran, 2003)

In summary mindfulness can be described as:

1. *"a powerful, momentary self-observation"* (Pandita and Wheeler, 2002)
2. a traditional form of meditation and a method of self-study.
3. a skill; it improves with practice.

4. undefended consciousness.
5. a way to practice surrendering.
6. a deliberate vulnerability, a chosen sensitivity.

In mindfulness, there is no intention to control what happens next. It is a deliberate relinquishing of control. That's why the first focus in traditional practice is often on the breath. To pay attention to the breath and not control it is more difficult than one might imagine, especially when we think about how little attention we ordinarily pay to breath and how well it works outside of our conscious control.

In mindfulness one focuses inward on the flow of one's experience.

One of the effects of practicing mindfulness is the gaining of perspective and distance on one's own internal world, as if one had stepped back and seen a larger canvas than before. One discovers how one habitually meets the world.

Francisco Varela and others have this to say about mindfulness:

> *"Here, then, we are dealing with two reversals of the most habitual cognitive functioning, of which the first is the condition for the second; the second cannot happen if the first has not already taken place.*
>
> - *A turning of the direction of attention from the exterior to the interior.*
> - *"A change in the quality of attention, which passes from the looking-for to the letting-come." (Depraz, Varela and Vermersch, 1999)*

How to Become Mindful

1. In Hakomi, we use it in small doses (30 seconds to a minute). We use it especially in the evocation of experiences.

2. We have many ways to help a client establish mindfulness. Here are some of the descriptions we use:

3. Please turn your attention inward to the flow of your present moment experience, including your body experience, your mental and emotional experience

4. Simply notice and allow

5. Quiet your mind by following your breath

6. Please notice what happens when I do this experiment, when I say these words to you…

7. Just allow your experiences to happen, without taking charge or trying to control anything

8. Be your own observer, notice what happens when I speak to this part of you

9. Please notice what happens spontaneously when I say…

How Mindfulness is Used in Evoking Reactions

"In a way, all successful psychotherapy depends on the ability to detach attention from habits and to describe them from the point of view of a neutral observer."   *(Palmer, 1988)*

The unique contribution of Hakomi is that the method contains, as a necessary element, precise experiments done with a person in a mindful state, the purpose being to evoke emotions, memories and reactions that will reveal or help access the implicit beliefs and early experiences and adaptations that are influencing the person's non-conscious, habitual behaviors.

If you can observe your own experience with a minimum of interference, and if you don't try to control what you experience, if you simply allow things to happen and you observe them, then you will be able to discover things about yourself that you did not know before. You can discover little pieces of the inner structures of your mind, the very things that make you who you are.

For example, I was at a conference in Vienna where I lectured to several hundred people. To demonstrate this method of using mindfulness, I did this. First, I asked them to predict something. I asked them to predict what their experience would be if they were in a state of mindfulness and I said to them, "You're a good person." I asked them to predict this while they were still in ordinary consciousness. Saying "you're a good person," while in mindfulness is a kind of experiment and I wanted them to think about what would happen when we did it. So, each person thought about it and told a neighbor what their predictions were. After that, I asked them to become quiet and turn inward (mindfulness). I gave them about thirty seconds to this and I talked to them in a very gentle, soothing voice about the various forms of experience they might notice: thoughts, emotions, memories, images, changes in muscle tension and breathing. Like that. After thirty seconds, I asked them to "Please notice your immediate reaction when you hear..." a slight pause, and then I, "You're a good person."

The results were these. About forty percent of the people reacted with experiences of sadness. Some felt a little sadness; some had tears; some cried. Another twenty-five percent or so experienced relief. A few people felt happy. Some noticed that their chests felt warmer and more open. Some had a thought or heard an inner voice that said things like, "No! I'm not!" About ninety percent failed to predict what actually happened. Ninety percent. That's why this method of self-study is so valuable. You learn things about yourself that you could not have predicted. A simple little experiment in mindfulness can do that. When an experiment is designed for one particular person, as happens in therapy, it can evoke some very powerful and revealing experiences.

Without mindfulness, it's possible nothing much would have been evoked. If you say, "You're a good person" to a person who isn't in mindfulness, isn't quietly turned inward and focused on the flow of his or her present experience, observing without interfering, the person might just reply casually, "Well, thanks!" If you ask it as a question, "Are you a good person," again without mindfulness, you might get an equally casual, emotionless answer, like, "Yes, I guess so." No sadness. No relief. No insight. Without mindfulness and the intention to study oneself, the person replies in an automatic, conversational way. Nothing very interesting happens. But, using mindfulness, with its open, self-observing concentration, something very important can easily happen.

How to Study and Report Your Reactions

Hakomi is assisted self-study. To make this process as easy as possible, a practitioner suggests doing little experiments while you are in a state of mindfulness. As a client, your responsibility is to allow, observe and report your reactions. Reactions will arise and die away by themselves if you do not allow them to lead into further actions. There is a difference between reactions and responses - as I use these terms, a reaction happens without conscious deliberation and a response happens with at least some conscious awareness.

As a client you want to signal to the therapist when you are ready for the experiment. When the experiment is done, just allow a reaction, observe it, without "becoming it," and stay with it for a few moments; be ready to report what you're noticing.

When you notice a reaction, report exactly what you noticed or are noticing if the reaction continues. Remember to report the experience. Meanings will reveal themselves if we stay with our experience.

Musings on the Self - What are We Observing?

"'I' has always been the magnificent mystery; I believe, I say, I whatever. But one must understand that there is no such tangible thing. It is just a particular mental state, a generated abstract entity we refer to as "I" or "self." So what is the self then? Well, it is a very important and useful construct, a complicated eigen (self) vector. It exists only as a calculated entity. Consider the following two examples of what I mean. First we have the concept of Uncle Sam. When one reads in the newspapers, "Uncle Sam bombards Belgrade," everyone understands that the U.S. Armed Forces have been deployed against that country.

> *However, there is no such entity as Uncle Sam. It is a convenient symbol and even a convenient concept that implies existence, but it is a category without elements. The "I" of the vortex, that which we work for and suffer for, is just a convenient word that stands for as global an event as does the concept of Uncle Sam vis-a-vis the reality of a complex, heterogeneous United States.*
>
> *The thalamocortical system is an isochronic sphere that synchronously relates the sensory-referred properties of the external world to internally generated motivations and memories. This temporally coherent event that binds, in the time domain, the fractured components of external and internal reality into a single construct is what we call the "self." ... the evolutionary development of a nervous system is an exclusive property of actively moving creatures."* (Llinás, 2002)

I am struck by the close resemblance of Llinás' statements to Buddhist ideas: *All is impermanent.* All is without a self. Llinás' says the self is just a particular mental state. In my mind that changes everything. The poet T.S. Elliot wrote, *"prepare a face to meet the faces that you meet."* So do we, prepare a mental state to meet (forgive me!) the mental states we meet? Or the mental states we anticipate meeting? I think that's close to the truth. We have and use situational selves, turned on and off automatically. And, there's also something that moves with us (and as us) from situation to situation. That may be the autobiographical memory and the temporal binding that needs to be there to have a self at all.

I can understand that the experience of no self, or to put a fine edge on it, no separate self, can be a life changing event. The sense of oneness that comes with it is a very highly prized state of mind. It entails a loss of boundaries and a sense of being connected to everything (see Newberg, D'Aquili and Rause, 2002). Hey, if it's just a mental state, why not change it? Isn't that exactly what we help clients do? We change their mental states, we change their minds. We change the way they habitually organize their interactions with the external world. We do not change their external worlds. We change the self that meets the world. We change the construct. And that changes everything.

> *"Prediction must be centralized—it leads to self. Given that prediction is the ultimate and most pervasive of all brain functions, one may ask how this function is grounded so that there evolved only one predictive organ. Intuitively, one can imagine the timing mismatches that would occur if there were more than one seat of prediction making judgment calls for a given organism's interaction with the world; it would be most disadvantageous for the head to predict one thing and the tail to predict another! For optimum efficiency it would seem that prediction must function to provide an unwavering residency and functional connectedness: it must somehow be centralized to the myriad interplays of the brain's strategies of interaction with the external world. We know this centralization of prediction as the abstraction we call the 'self.'"*   *(Llinás, 2002)*

So, according to Llinás, it is the self that generates a unifying order out of the buzzing mess around us. The self, he says, is the centralization of prediction. It binds our world together into one thing we can deal with. It creates order and it does so through temporal synchronicity. And we know prediction of demand is one of the greatest influences on physiology and behavior (see Sterling, 2004).

The operative self, the one we can witness doing things and saying things, is the external manifestation of a set of habits, memories and implicit and explicit beliefs. We search for external indicators of these to help us understand how a person is organizing his or her experiences and behavior. And also we use indicators to do little experiments in mindfulness. We are attempting to do two things with all this: (1) we're trying to resolve and integrate old, emotionally painful memories and (2) we're trying to make implicit beliefs conscious, in order to challenge them and change them into more realistic and satisfying ones. In this way, we change the self, as concept, as mental state, as centralized predictor.

Loving Presence

> This essay was originally written in 2010 for the Training Handbook

The Therapist's State of Mind

"In this model, what is seen as primary in shaping experience is not external reality—not what is cognized, not the object of awareness—but rather the properties of that moment of mind itself."
(Goleman, 1991)

The phrase 'state of mind' has much more precise meaning nowadays than it had just a few decades ago. Neurological research has revealed much about exactly what states the brain can be in when people interact (see Lewis et al, 2001; Ogden, 2015, Porges, 2011). Many books have been written on the interaction of caregivers and the infants in their care (Ogden, 2015). Adults in relationship also affect each others' states of mind. For the very intimate relationship between a therapist and client, the therapist's conscious awareness and deliberate control of his or her state of mind is essential. The effect of the therapist's state of mind on the process of this method is without doubt the single most important factor in its success.

To best serve others in their self-study, the therapist must be able to sustain both presence and compassion. The therapist has to maintain a constant focus on present activity and present experience, both her own and that of the client. That kind of presence is needed. A feeling of compassion is also essential. When presence and compassion are combined and constant, the therapist's state of mind can be called loving presence. In training people in this method, the development and practice of this state of mind are primary goals. In a very short time, loving presence can establish in the client, a sense of being safe, cared for, heard and understood. Self-exploration, especially when using mindfulness, places clients in extremely vulnerable positions. A therapist in loving presence helps clients to allow this vulnerability and

Loving Presence

provides the best context for assisted self-study to happen. Here's a quote:

> *"Loving presence is easy to recognize. Imagine a happy and contented mother looking at the sweet face of her peaceful newborn.*
>
> *She is calm, loving and attentive. Unhurried and undistracted, the two of them seem to be outside of time... simply being. Gently held within a field of love and life's wisdom, they are as present with each other as any two could be." (Kurtz)*

For the therapist to develop this state of mind, he or she must first of all look at others as living beings and sources of inspiration. As one therapist put it:

> *"If you cannot see anything lovable in this person that you can respond to in a genuine way, then you are not the right person to help this person." (Brenman-Gibson, 1992).*

It is this intention and habit of seeing something lovable in the other that creates the feeling state necessary for loving presence. The first thing I instruct students to do: create this habit as the primary thing in any interaction! Create it and sustain it throughout your sessions!

> *"I want to start with the most important thing I have to say: The essence of working with another person is to be present as a living being. And this is lucky, because if we had to be smart, or good, or mature, or wise, then we would probably be in trouble. But, what matters is not that. What matters is to be a human being with another human being, to recognize the other person as another being in there. Even if it is a cat or a bird, if you are trying to help a wounded bird, the first thing you have to know is that there is somebody in there, and that you have to wait for that "person", that being in there, to be*

> *in contact with you. That seems to me to be the most important thing. »*   *(Gendlin, 1990)*

How do we support this intention? The first goal is to establish a relationship that will support self-study; the habit of gathering information by asking questions and considering answers is not the way to do it. First, one must avoid being drawn into a conversation about abstractions—ideas, explanations, the meaning of the past and such. The therapist's words and actions must demonstrate that he or she is paying attention to what the client is experiencing right now, cares about what the client is feeling, and understands what that means for the client. This connection through present experience is the key to limbic resonance. So, the therapist searches for what there is about the client that is emotionally nourishing or inspiring. She practices appreciation and connection. Another thing that helps build the right relationship is realizing the process as a collaborative enterprise where feelings of partnership, teamwork and mutual respect are basic. The idea that we are not separate, that we are inescapably parts of a whole greater than each of us alone, is the root of loving presence.

> This essay was originally written by Ron for his Readings 2010 collection

Loving Presence

> *"Vocal communication between a mammal and offspring is universal. Remove a mother from her litter of kittens or puppies and they begin an incessant yowling—the separation cry—whose shrill distress drills into the ear of any normal human being. But take a baby Komodo dragon away from its scaly progenitor, and it stays quiet. Immature Komodos do not broadcast their presence because Komodo adults are avid cannibals. A lifesaving vacuum of silence stretches between a reptilian mother and young. Advertising vulnerability makes sense only for those animals whose brains can conceive of a parental protector." (Lewis et al, 2001)*

When someone maintains loving presence with another, it has a powerful effect. Possibly without even noticing it, the other feels safer, cared for and understood. When this happens in a therapeutic relationship, healing has already begun.

Loving presence is a state of being. It is pleasant, good for your health, rewarding in and of itself. It's a state in which you feel open hearted and well intentioned. In its purest form, it is spiritually nourishing and sensitive to subtleties. It is the best state to be in when you are offering emotional support. One look around will tell you that this kind of support is needed everywhere. A healthy emotional life requires a safe place to express feelings and someone loving to bear witness. It requires the release of old hurts and an opening to new paths to happiness. Loving presence is emotional support and it is an important part of relating to others. It can make a big difference in our lives. In psychotherapy, it is essential.

Loving Presence

People learn about relating through experience. Our earliest experiences create templates for the kinds of relationships we will be capable of. If the early experiences lacked real love and care, we're not likely to enjoy that later in life, unless we do something to change this early programming, unless we discover new ways of connecting.

Loving presence is first of all about being in the present, showing up. It's about being focused on what is happening in the moment on both your own experience and the experiences of the one you're with. It is an opening and an exchange. It is not grounded in ideas or even words. It is an emotional connection made between the nervous systems of two people that asks us to surrender.

> *"Because our minds seek one another through limbic resonance, because our physiologic rhythms answer to the call of limbic regulation, because we change one another's brains through limbic revision – what we do inside relationship matters more than any other aspect of human life"*
> *(Lewis et all, 2001)*

> *"There is no compassion without humor; no love without pleasure no freedom without enlightenment." (Da Free John)*

No love without pleasure. If we want to be in loving presence, we need to find pleasure in being with people. How do we do that? How do we get pleasure from being with someone? We have to search for it. We have to deliberately take the time to search for what there is about this person we're with that makes us feel good. We have to search for what there is about this person that inspires us. This searching and finding has to become a habit and our first priority.

It helps if we learn to stay calm. Being calm allows us to take our time, not busy doing something else, not worrying or solving problems. We have to be sitting pretty squarely in the middle of non-achievement. We cannot be trying to accomplish anything. We need to avoid straining. We have to look out for pride and need for approval, recognition or perfection. We have to be able to slow down. Being calm helps us to be sensitive and open to enjoyment.

It can be esthetic pleasure. We may be able to see the people we're with as beautiful, like a wonderful painting. When we start to see them that way, the whole space we share with them starts to change. Or we can sense their strength of character, their integrity, their intelligence or sense of humor. There can be pleasure in each of those.

Or we can start with very simple pleasures, like interest and curiosity. From there we can move on to the fun of working with the mystery and complexity of human behavior. Then we may become aware of the honor and privilege of being present with and part of someone's powerful inner work. And there's also the beauty and courage of the human spirit.

In loving presence we move from egocentric to non-egocentric pleasures. We move away from our own importance to loving the other. We learn to drift with someone into a loving place. Sometimes, that's all we have to do to give someone the emotional support they need. It's as if we simply offer our love to people and they start to heal. It all just unfolds right in front of us!

It is easy to be present, if we're not busy doing something else. Most of the time, however, we're not only busy doing something else, we're doing a lot of it automatically, habitually, and unconsciously. Typically, as helping professionals, especially counselors and psychotherapists, we believe we are helping others solve their problems. We're task-oriented. We want to make something happen for our clients. As a result, we work too hard. This focus on doing and making things happen draws us away from loving presence.

We might need to explore how our self-image gets in the way. The kind of pleasure and nourishment we're talking about here is not nourishment for the ego. It's nourishment for something deeper, something much older. We need to find something bigger in ourselves. In order to be helpful to anyone, whether as a therapist or just as a friend, loving presence is the best place to start. When we are compassionate, present, sensitive and appreciative, good things start to happen. It's true. There are things to do. We want good things to happen for our clients. Loving presence, in spite of its quiet inactivity, provides the very best context for that.

The pleasure one can get out of being in the role of helper is the pleasure of comforting, of being close, of seeing clearly, being real, understanding and helping someone else understand, helping someone become more alive and more free.

> *"The vocation of psychotherapy confers a few unexpected fringe benefits on its practitioners... it impels participation in a process that our modern world has all but forgotten: sitting in a room with another person for hours at a time with no purpose in mind but attending. As you do so, another world expands and comes alive to your senses." (Lewis et al., 2001).*

Love and presence are about finding joy in this work. It's the best reason for doing it.

Contact and Tracking

> Contact and tracking are essential skills in the Hakomi Method. Although both skills were integral parts of the original method, Ron refined his ideas about these two elements over the course of his career.

Contact

I will give you some history.

Carl Rogers developed a unique method of psychotherapy, usually called, surprisingly enough, Rogerian Therapy. He described it as person centered. His idea was to take what clients said that was emotionally charged and do two things: he'd name the person's experience in a sympathetic voice, possibly restate what had been said in simpler, less charged language. Those simpler, calmer restatements came to be called contact statements. For example, a client might say, in an excited voice, "I'm really worried about the kids playing in the street. The kids are out there and there are cars going by!" To which Rogers might reply, "That's really scary isn't it? You'd like to see the kids have a safer place to play." The result might be that the person would feel heard, might calm down, might move deeper into his/her emotions, or might decide to do something about the situation. Somehow, all Rogers had to do was to reflect back what the person was saying in a calmer, clearer way. Very often, Rogers was naming what the person was experiencing. ("That's really scary." "That makes you sad.") That, plus a lot of insight and a depth of kindness, was Rogerian therapy. Rogers wrote books, he taught and did workshops and his method became popular, especially in Europe.

Rogers did a very significant experiment. He trained secretaries to do "Rogerian therapy". The result was, on average they did better than trained psychotherapists. This was a very surprising outcome. Because Rogers chose secretaries who had very warm personalities, the people who were clients in those experiments reported that they were more satisfied with the secretaries than with the professionals. The clients didn't know they were secretaries. Others have made similar findings.

I get two things from all that: Warmth counts! And clients will move through their healing processes, if they have support for an awareness of their own experiences.

I distinguish between contact statements per se and a relational state of being in contact. That is, therapist and client form a relationship where there is a sense of connection with each other, a "being with" each other. Therapist and client are continuously aware of each other. In that state, the client feels heard, attended to and understood. The client senses that the therapist is aware of what he or she is experiencing. (Remember: warmth counts!) Being in contact is being in it together, as opposed to being separate or alone. This feeling has a powerful influence on the client's emotions and behavior. Think of babies crying and wanting to be held! Someone comes, picks the infant up, holds it gently and speaks to it in a soothing voice. The infant's situation has changed radically. That's the state of being in contact. Contact statements are one of the ways we get there.

Contact statements help dissolve the distance between people and the isolation they feel. Contact statements convey to the client that you're really listening and following what's going on with them. And, if you also happen to be one of Rogers' hand-picked secretaries or just a warm person, the client will feel safer.

So, if you can be in loving presence and make good contact statements once in a while, this will happen: You will convey to the client that you're compassionate, present, and that you understand what's going on. With that kind of support, the client will move through his or her healing process with much greater ease and satisfaction. Quicker, too!

When the client feels contacted, the situation may also feel unique. Meher Baba used to say, *"I can love you better than you can love yourself."* We can be present with clients better than they can be with themselves. That's our job. If we do it well, then we're helping to create the best situation for the client's self-study. Often, just one good contact statement, will start a powerful process. New clients usually don't expect things like that to happen. But they do because, at some level, the client is realizing: Somebody's really there! This person is really listening! This person understands... is sympathetic... is compassionate! I'm not being judged!

You don't have to make contact statements to have that happen. You can look like you're listening. You can nod in the right places. You can have a sympathetic look on your face, so that when the person looks at you, they see that you are present, that you are getting it. It doesn't have to be verbal at all. Somebody's sad and you make a sympathetic sound. People make contact with babies all the time. Animals, too! It's the tone of voice; the position of your head; the fact that you're looking at them; the fact that you are quiet and patient, not interrupting; not arguing; your relaxed posture. All of those things convey the same information: you're friendly and you're interested in them. It also helps if sometimes you make a short simple contact statement like, when tears begin to form, you say, "Sad, huh."

Contact does several things. The first is, as I've said, it creates a safe, inviting context for emotional healing. Second, it helps determine what will be the focus of attention. Realistically, there may be several things that you could contact. If you contact the person's present experience, you're helping them make the choice to focus on that. A client might come in and say, "You know, I had a really bad thing happen." You could say, "Oh, what was it?" Or, you could say, "You're in a lot of pain, aren't you." You're making a choice. If you're aware, you make a conscious choice (to go with the client's present experience). I might ask, "What was that bad thing that happened?" And then the client might just start telling me all about it. "Well, you know, a couple of days ago...." And we're into a story and very likely the present painful experience that was there for a moment will dissipate with the talking. The client talks himself right out of his present experience. Whereas the contact statement, "You're in a lot of pain...." could shift attention to the pain, deepening the emotion, moving the process towards deeper material.

So, when you respond to a client, you're making subtle choices about what to focus on. You're telling the client what you're paying attention to, in effect suggesting that he or she do the same. We have to realize that we're doing that. We're influencing the process. We

Contact and Tracking

don't determine the process, but we influence it. One of the ways we do that is by making contact statements.

We influence the process, but we don't initially direct it. When we make a contact statement we're following the client's process even though we're selecting what to contact. The client decides what they will do next. We wait for that. After a contact statement, we wait to see what the client will do next. We don't start by running things. At some point we may start directing, but in the beginning, we want to help clients go where they have to go. At some level, clients know where that is. If you make good contact statements, at the right times, client's will take themselves where they have to go. It's just like having a conversation. The person says something to you and you say something that indicates to the person, yeah, I got that. Yeah I know what you just said. So now, it's their choice to go with what they want to tell you next. If you make good contact then the person moves. The process moves.

Here's when you want to make contact statements: when you see a shift in the person's state of mind, or a change in the person's emotional state. You want to contact the shifts. That's really important. Any time you notice a shift, a quick, quiet contact statement will help. Remember that present experience takes priority. When it shifts, contact it! Statements like this are what I mean: "That felt good, huh?" or, "Feeling sad now, huh?" or, "Just had a thought?" (You can always put the "huh" part in the tone of your voice.) Or, "You're remembering something." You're contacting shifts in emotions and states of mind. That moves the process along.

The reason this method is so fast is that we don't try to completely control it. We're just helping it go where it wants to go. If you set the process up so that you're completely in charge, the client becomes passive and his or her internally driven inclinations are not allowed to flourish. If you take the position that you have to lead, you'll run into all kinds of overt and covert resistance. I search for and follow what wants to happen. As it says in the Tao Te Ching, "The best leader follows."

Contact is my way of influencing the process without taking charge. By contacting, I let the person know, "Okay, I got that, you can tell me the next thing. You can go on to the thing you want to say or need to do." I'm telling the client, "I followed you on that step. What's the next step?" As a result, we're dancing so smoothly, you can't tell who's in charge. Contact greases the tracks. Being in contact and making appropriate contact statements, at the right time, without doing anything else, sets the process moving towards both present experience and spontaneous expression.

The best contact statements are very simple statements. Although there are other kinds of contact statements—like the ones that summarize the content of what the client has been saying—the ones that are the most powerful are the ones that simply name present experience. By naming present experience you move the client's attention towards his or her immediate experiences. Summary contact directs attention to what the person's talking about. Like this: "Oh, so this is about the time you got angry huh?" You're contacting the content. Or, after the person has been talking for three or four minutes, you summarize that with something like this: "So, this is about all the times you were sad." That's a summary contact statement. It's good. It's useful and does much the same as far as communicating to the client that you understand. But, it's not as powerful, not as influential, as contacting present experience. Experience is not just emotions. It could be something like: "You're remembering that now, huh?" Remembering is an experience.

When we talk about contact, we're including both a state of being in contact, and a statement that helps create contact. In that state of being, you could say the client feels contacted. Or they're affected in such a way that even without thinking about it, they know you are giving them your complete attention. If you offer your complete attention to somebody, if you're really present and they recognize that—even without thinking about it—that affects them. It's a signal that tells the person that there's somebody else there who's involved in what's happening with them, who's following what's going on, who has some understanding of what's going on and cares. All of that is part of contact. It's a very different situation when you begin a relationship with the intention to make contact rather than the intention to simply gather information about a person's problem. The relationship is totally different. If your intention is to make contact, you're creating the setting in which this person can unfold, can open up emotionally. It's not an abstract process where somebody describes his problem and you analyze it, diagnose it, and recommend a treatment or give some advice. It's not problem solving. It's a whole different way of relating. This method starts with contact; it starts with establishing a relationship in which the person feels safe and understood. Loving presence partly takes care of that signaling. Contact statements do the rest.

When you make a contact statement you're signalling the person. You're demonstrating that you are present and that you understand. This creates a relationship that's very different from the ones we usually have. We're not going fast. We're not being busy and getting things done. Our focus isn't "What's the problem?" Our intention isn't to find a solution. We're not concerned with who's right. We don't argue or debate. We really listen as well as we can. We work to establish a special kind of relationship, one in which mental-emotional healing has a good chance to unfold. For building that kind of relationship contact statements are essential.

Tracking - The Steps: Where Attention Goes

Let's go through the steps of the process. The psychotherapeutic work I'm describing here requires paying attention to a few different things in quick succession. To do that, you can't be totally focused on any one of them to the exclusion of the others. In normal interactions, we concentrate on the content of the conversation and in effect become entranced by it. Sharing attention among several things eventually becomes a habit. We call this training of attention 'tracking'.

In the beginning, however, one has to acquire these rather special habits of attending. So, in the training we deliberately practice paying attention to five specific aspects of the client's behavior. I'll name each of them now and describe them in detail as we go along.

First, you're looking for something about the client that inspires compassion and appreciation, something that makes you feel good. That's how you create and maintain a state of loving presence.

Second, you're attending to the outward signs of the client's present experience. You're taking notice of the nonverbal signs that suggest what the client might be experiencing each moment.

Third, you must follow the conversation without losing your attention to it entirely.

The fourth type of tracking is difficult to describe. It's about getting a general sense of what kind of person the client is. It's more general than tracking the client's present experience. It's his or her unique way of being with all the personal traits and characteristics. You're attending to those things, whatever they are, that somehow give you ideas about and a feel for who the client is at a deep level. All the character theories have words for categorizing people—oral, anal, phallic, hysteric, psychopathic, rigid, borderline, insecure, disorganized, schizoid, and on and on. They're all general categories. Some are about pathology; some are about adapting to the unavoidable conditions of existence. All are ways one can practice thinking about people. Sometimes, knowing those concepts will put you in the ballpark of understanding a client quickly. But, in general, they won't help you very much in the moment to moment decisions that are the essence of doing attuned therapy. To do therapy well, you have to be able to use present behavior in precise ways to contact, relate and to support discovery. You need precise ideas about what emotions, beliefs, images, and ideas are running your client's life right now and in general. You need to discover what events shaped her present experience, her habits and her way of being. To help clients know themselves, you have to know them first, at least in part, and with more precision than character theories provide. Sure, there are common traits amongst people, but for fast, effective therapy, it is more helpful to have poetic sensibilities and a sharp eye for the fine grain.

This fourth step is getting a feel for the client's world. What are the underlying, probably unconscious rules that shape his experience and behavior? That's what you need to know in order to help the client discover who he is and how he got that way.

If as Llinas (2002) says we are basically dreaming machines: what kind of reality is this person dreaming? So we can ask: what kind of reality is this person dreaming?

All of this searching (tracking) is preparation for creating experiments in mindfulness that will help the client discover how he organizes his experiences, what the rules are, what his core beliefs are. The client discovers the key memories that determined the rules and beliefs. The therapist doesn't have to know these things in detail. He only has to know enough to create the experiments that will help the client discover them. The therapist as scientist has to be a good guesser. And then do those little experiments in mindfulness that are unique to Hakomi.

So, not only do you track for moment to moment changes—as part of being present with and contacting the client—you also look for what doesn't change. You look for 'who they are,' something characteristic, something that suggests it is connected to the deeper patterns and rules that govern this person's experience and behavior. You look for style and manner.

The fifth thing we do with our attention is: we search for indicators. These are not as general as character. These are specific habits. An indicator can be any observable habit. It could be a posture, like the angle at which the person holds her head. Or a gesture or a way of moving. It could be the facial expression that's always there, or a tone of voice. You're looking and listening for something that might be useful as part of an experiment. You're looking for clues to core material. Indicators are used to bring core material into consciousness. The experiments we do with them move the process into the expression of emotions and they bring the organizing levels of the mind into awareness.

If you can be aware of these five loci of attention at the same time, your work will become creative, exciting and effective. So, it's important to get to the point where you're attending to all these things automatically and without effort. To prioritize these five:

1. look for something in the other that supports your loving presence;
2. track for signs of the other's present experience;
3. follow the conversation;
4. get the feel of the whole person; and
5. search for indicators.

The reasons for these priorities are these: loving presence is the emotional fuel for the whole enterprise; it is the essence of healthy and healing relationships. Without it, nothing very significant is likely to happen. It's the first thing you want to establish. Tracking and contacting present experience help create the right relationship for healing. They let the client know you're paying attention and that you understand what's going on. Following the conversation is the normal thing to do, so... Follow it, but don't get into a trance about the content. Don't allow the ideas being presented to become the total focus of your attention.

Getting a sense of the whole person, through skillful observation of the non-verbal communications and indicators allows you to consciously adjust to and respond to who this particular person is. This will affect the relationship in a powerful way and it will provide ideas for experiments and insights into what kind of emotional nourishment the client has difficulty taking in (missing experiences).

Indicators

> The concept of indicators was one of the last refinements of Hakomi. Instead of using character strategies to create hypotheses and experiments, Ron developed and taught his student to track for indicators because there are unlimited numbers of them and they all hold the potential for good experiments.

Indicators

Remember, you're doing a lot of things at once. You are studying the client's behavior for something interesting, something that might be connected to a core belief. To find indicators, you follow the flow of nonverbal expression. Or, you sense what kind of experience you're having with this client right now. You're following what's happening in general and in particular, and you're finding words for that, noting what's interesting in it all. It could be a gesture, a facial expression, almost anything that is somehow part of being with this person. Some examples are the habit of telling stories or the habit of editing their own speech. You're on the lookout for a piece of behavior or an element of style or anything that suggests it may have a connection to character, early memories, or a particular emotions. So, you are looking for indicators.

This is how the process starts: conversation, loving presence, tracking and contact, getting a feel for the client's personality and searching for indicators. This first phase continues for a while (awhile being anywhere from a few minutes to several sessions). The process can't proceed to the next step, finding indicators and thinking of little experiments, until the first phase has done two things, (1) the client feels safe and has confidence in the therapist, and (2), you've gotten an idea about an indicator and an experiment to do with it. While you've been establishing that sense of safety and understanding for the client, you've been searching for an indicator. With a little experience doing this, you'll be able to find lots of good indicators. The more experience, the easier it becomes. It's mostly an intuitive process, sensing that there is a message in a piece of behavior and learning to read those messages.

Working with Indicators

Doing a therapy session means doing many things at once. Besides getting and staying in loving presence, following the conversation, tracking the client's present experience and making contact statements, right from the beginning, I search for indicators. With practice, you can get to a point where your adaptive unconscious handles almost everything. Just as it does to become expert at anything, being able to multi-task like that takes a lot of practice (see Brooks, 2009; Gladwell, 2008).

When the adaptive unconscious is able to handle those other tasks, the practitioner has time to find and think about indicators. The first thing to think about an indicator that you've found would be: what kinds of adaptations and beliefs does it express. After you have an idea about that, you'll want to think of an experiment you can create to work with it.

Here's what an indicator is. It is an habitual behavior of some kind, usually nonverbal and almost always done automatically, outside of awareness. Indicators are clues as to what sort of situations the person faced in her life and how she acted to deal those situations. Indicators are external signs of adaptations made to emotionally charged situations, made either consciously and deliberately or, when very young, procedurally.

Working with indicators means this: you search for some quality or little habit the client has. It should be something interesting to you, something you sense could be connected to an adaptation and/or a core belief. Some indicators are fairly common. You've seen a lot of them, even if you didn't consciously register them. And, if you have experience with Hakomi, you probably know some from practicing, reading and watching sessions. You may even know some experiments to do with particular indicators. In the course of practicing you'll discover other indicators. If, like me, you enjoy thinking about people, working with indicators should be very satisfying. After a while, you should become quite good at getting the meaning of the indicators you come across.

Shifting Your Own Attention

Of course, at some point in the process, we shift the client's attention to an indicator. Before that though, we have to shift our own attention to the "realm" of the indicators: the client's present behaviors and nonverbal expressions. There are some indicators that appear in the client's story, like themes, attitudes, reports of intense experiences, but these are very likely to be well known to the client and very likely not the best routes to unconscious core material. Habits, which lie outside of conscious awareness and which are not controlled by conscious intention, are much more likely to reflect unconscious core material.

Some of our attention is on the story. We need to follow what the client is saying because not to would have a disastrous effect on the relationship. Also, it can be very useful to note unusually strong words and phrases. So, attention to the story is necessary and useful at times. But, more useful and absolutely necessary, is attention to the nonverbal aspects and micro-expressions of the client. Micro-expressions, those facial expressions and gestures that take place very quickly, some in less than half a second, can be indicators of at least two things: one, they can be signs of the client's present experience. As such, they are very useful for making contact statements. The second thing they can express is a conscious or unconscious nonverbal "comment" on what's being said. Again, they are good for making contact statements, but they can also be clues to deeper material.

It's especially important to attend to those nonverbal behaviors that seem to be habitual and a little unusual. These almost always have links to unconscious material. Because they're habits, they operate non-consciously, and being outside of awareness, the client won't bring attention to them. The therapist has to bring attention to it before an experiment in mindfulness can be suggested. That's why we have to shift the client's attention. But, before we can do that, we must have seen or heard it ourselves. So, our own attention can't just be on the story. We've got to pay attention to the storyteller.

This kind of attention is exactly the kind one needs to create harmonious relationships. It's being more concerned with the person,

Indicators

more attentive to the present lived experience of another being. It is the foundation of limbic resonance and loving presence. It is concrete, timely, rich with feeling and direct understanding, and it is a primary source of compassion, humor and delight.

Shifting the Client's Attention to the Indicator

Once all that is established, the next step can be taken: switching the client's attention to the indicator. To make the switch, you may have to interrupt the client; you could be switching to something that the client isn't conscious of. That could be disorienting. It helps if the client has experience with the method and understands what the therapist is doing. If the client knows that the goal is self-discovery and that the therapist is there to support that, then the switching attention to an indicator is accepted and not experienced as an interruption. But, don't switch to an indicator until you have an experiment in mind. Otherwise, the whole process just hangs there.

The keys are timing, tone and topic. Timing is about finding an easy opening, a place in the conversation where you have an opportunity to switch. Tone is about your sensitivity to the possible disruption you might cause, using soft tone and gentle language. Topic is about finding something that's probably going to be interesting to the client. That usually depends on how significant it really is and how surprising for the client. Again, practice makes this step easy and useful.

To shift attention to an indicator, you can say something like: 'You know what I notice about you?' Or: 'There is something I'm finding really interesting about you.' Something like that. Whatever the conversation is about, when it seems right, shift attention to the indicator. Whatever it is: the way the client moves her hand; the way her face looks; the way she's breathing; something she says, some repetitive theme in the conversation. Here's an example: you notice that the client always keeps her head tilted to one side or the other. You think it's interesting and if you've had some experience with it, you know it's a good indicator to work with. It's usually about doubt and mistrust, with some memories of being betrayed and emotionally hurt. As an experiment, you decide you'll ask the client to move her head slowly into the vertical. So, at the right time, you say to her, 'You know, I've noticed something about you that might be interesting to experiment with. It's the fact that your head is always tilted to one side or the other. Can we do an experiment with that?' She says, 'Yes.' You ask for mindfulness and a signal and you do the experiment.

With the woman I worked with recently, I noticed she was moving her hand, her left hand, with a jabbing motion, as she talked about her father. I pointed that out and, as an experiment, we took over holding her hand back and that's how we accessed her anger. That was our experiment: holding her hand back. The result was, she felt her anger and suddenly became very fearful, and the memories of being terrified of her father took her over. With that in consciousness, we helped her calm down and realize, she was no longer in danger from him. He had passed away years ago. He was still living in my client's mind and habits, still making her afraid of her own anger. So, the rule was: don't allow anger. The belief was: it will get you a terrible beating.

Indicators as Data for Experiments

The purpose of the whole process of using indicators to develop experiments is three-fold:
  (1) to help the therapist understand the client
  (2) to help the client understand him or herself
  (3) when appropriate, to evoke a healing process

Often, when I talk about the meaning of an indicator, I use the word "modelling". I use it in the sense of making a theoretical model in your own mind about what memories, adaptations, and beliefs could explain the particular indicator you're observing. That's how science works: get some data, create a theory about it, and find a way to test the theory. If you can't do something to corroborate a theory (meaning, test it), it's not much good. You can have a lot of ideas about a client, but you'll need some way to test them. We call those tests "experiments". As they say about jazz, "it don't mean a thing, if it ain't got that swing."

Below are a set of examples of indicators as data; the ideas about what the indicator means (theory, model); the kinds of experiments one might do to test the theory; and the kinds of outcomes that support or fail to support the theory.

Three Examples of Indicators:

Indicator: talks fast.
- Model: memories of not given time and attention.
- Belief: must get thoughts across to people quickly.
- Adaptation: talk fast.
- Verbal Experiments: "I have time for you." "I'm listening."
- Experiment suggestion: talk slowly.
- Possible Outcomes: relief, sadness, memories of not being listened to, tension.

Indicator: head held at an angle, turned away, eyes not looking directly at therapist.
- Model: memories of being lied to, tricked, manipulated.
- Belief: you can't trust people to tell you the truth.

Indicators

- Adaptation: distrust.
- Verbal experiment : "You can trust me," "I won't lie to you."
- Physical experiment : falling backward and being caught or taking the weight of the arm.
- Possible outcomes: relief, thoughts like "no I can't" (meaning, "can't trust"), "bullshit!", memories of being lied to, etc., fear, tension

Indicator: shrugs shoulders.
- Model: memories of being blamed.
- Belief: people will try to make you feel guilty.
- Adaptation: express innocence and/or ignorance.
- Verbal experiment: "It wasn't your fault," "I don't blame you."
- Physical experiment: take over burdened shoulders.
- Possible Outcomes: emotionally charged expression of anger.

Results of Experiments:

If the experiment gets no reaction, it probably means the model is incorrect.

As an outcome of an experiment, relief indicates that the experimental content was nourishing and taken in. This is not the kind of outcome that will generally lead to a healing process. Healing processes are generally about emotional-spiritual nourishment that is difficult or impossible to take in. Spiritual nourishment means that which supports the full human development of a person towards love and freedom.

Nonverbal Indicators and Formative Experiences

Accessing the kinds of beliefs that pervasively and unconsciously influence experience requires that the therapist get ideas about what the client's formative early experiences were or what implicit beliefs the client's behaviors are expressing. To gather this information, the therapist focuses attention on the qualities of the client's habitual posture, tone of voice, facial expressions, gestures, eye contact, speech patterns and such. A few examples would be: ending verbal statements with the inflection of a question or an habitually sad looking face or tilt of the head.

Many of these qualities are habitual nonverbal expressions of implicit beliefs. We call them indicators. As you may imagine, there are many such indicators. Some can be completely obvious as to what they say about the client. Others require that the therapist learn them over time. In Bioenergetics, for example, the indicators are often postural. A sunken chest and locked knees for a Bioenergetic therapist would be indicators of *"an oral pattern"* (Lowen, 1972). Given that pattern, the therapist has both a diagnosis and a way to proceed with treatment. Almost all methods of psychotherapy use particular sets of indicators this way and usually refer to them as symptoms. In this method, we use indicators differently. We use them to get ideas for experiments.

As we interact and relate to others, we don't normally focus on their little, seemingly insignificant habits. In an ordinary interaction, conversation is most important; we might not consciously think about a person's subtle nonverbal behaviors. We might ignore a slight feeling of discomfort that results from the way the other person is looking at us with her head always turned to one side. Odds are she won't be consciously aware of either the angle of her head or the skepticism it indicates. This level of interaction is usually handled by the adaptive unconscious. In Hakomi, we consciously search for indicators and the turning of the head is a common one.

Through experimenting with it many times, I have come to expect that it can indicate formative experiences of not being told the truth or not being understood. The emotion associated with it is usually hurt. Though the hurt is not being felt at the moment, it is an expression of the implicit belief: "I must be careful about what people are telling me! I could get hurt again." Though not conscious, the message is clear in the non-verbal expressions.

Indicators are the external expressions of this process. In Hakomi, we use indicators to create experiments, experiments designed to trigger reactions. This is a vital piece of the method. It is our clear intention to study a client's behavior not for symptoms of disease but for sources of experiments. We anticipate that the experiments we carry out will bring the unconscious, adaptive processes driving that behavior into the client's awareness. A therapist using this approach is thought of as having an experimental attitude. We are evidence seekers, evidence which is gathered on the spot, evidence that clients can use to understand themselves. The basic idea is this:

1. indicators suggest experiments;
2. experiments create reactions;
3. reactions are evidence of implicit beliefs.

Gathering evidence is what experiments are all about and that's exactly why we do them. For instance, if the client's habit is to hold her head a little bit off center and turned slightly away, we might do an experiment where the client, while in a mindful state, slowly turns her head back towards center. Most clients, when doing this movement deliberately and carefully will react with fear. This fear is about being emotionally hurt and it is associated with memories of that happening and beliefs about how to avoid it. The habitual turning of the head is only one indicator and the experiment only one of many possibilities. There are endless numbers of possible indicators and the experiments that can be done. Finding indicators and devising suitable experiments is one of the things that makes this work so interesting. It is a combination of searching for clues like a detective and testing them like a scientist. It is a long way from "the talking cure".

> This is a very small list of indicators as Ron preferred not to give lists but for people to make guesses about what they observe.

Examples of Indicators

Examples of a few Indicators	Possible Meanings
Head nodding, eyes checking	Do you get it? Reaching for understanding
Head turned to one side or tilted	Doubt, disbelief, mistrust
Chin thrust forward	Challenge, stubbornness
Chin held high	Unaffected, superior, avoidance of feelings
Eyes always searching	Vigilance, fear, trauma
Eyes usually closed	Not wanting to be interrupted
Many self-interruptions	Fear of making mistakes
Voice very soft	Low energy, blocked emotions
Pace of speech fast	Not sure attention will last, not enough time
Self editing one's speech	Not being acceptable, expecting judgment
Question marks at the end of speech	Not being understood, not ok to be alive
Facial expression (when relaxed)	General mood, usual emotion or basic attitude
Shrugging of shoulders	"It's not my fault", feeling blamed
Hands making fists	Anger, defense
Sighing	Sadness, frustration
Immediate disagreement	Protective of own opinions
Caved-in chest	Defeat, resignation, giving up
Arching back	Self-reliant
Rigid, tight, contained	Not allowed to express emotions, fear of violence

Experiments

Two essays about experiments and experimental mind. Ron regarded precise experiments in mindfulness to be one of the unique contributions of Hakomi to the field of psychotherapy.

Please note that Ron originally used the term "probe" to mean a particular type of experiment. We now use the term "verbal experiment."

> From the Readings 2010

Experiments 1st Essay

By pursuing the deeper levels of belief, by wanting to know what habits and convictions are influencing the client's emotions, thoughts and behaviors, we lead clients towards consciousness, understanding their deep material. It's not just our curiosity; it's our method. We don't just ask for the information we're after; in most cases, we don't even know what to ask. We don't just ask questions. Questioning has its difficulties. It doesn't usually yield the kind of information we're after. It often evokes speculation and explanation. Questioning creates an interview type atmosphere, leaving the client passive and thoughtful. Experiments, on the other hand, almost always evoke the memories, images and beliefs that exist at the deeper levels. So, in order to bring into consciousness what was unconscious, we satisfy our curiosity by being detectives and scientists. We think and we experiment. We work that way to get the information we want and the client needs. All our techniques serve that end.

I did supervision last week. Several people there were teacher level. I noticed that there's something important that I hadn't yet gotten across strongly enough. It was pretty clear to everyone that loving presence is a big part of the work. It's essential and it takes a certain quality of personality. (We all have it, thank heaven.) And, it's only part of the work. The other part of the work is a set of attitudes and skills that are needed for what the whole method is built around, the central thing that the method hinges on, the fulcrum: the experiments. The discoveries that clients make are the outcomes of experiments. It's what we do that others don't do. At least I don't know of any other therapy process that does experiments in mindfulness. These little probes and things we do, they're like assisted moments of insight. We set them up carefully. We prepare the client. We wait for the exactly right moment. When everything's ready, we carefully do whatever it is. Then we watch for and ask for the outcome: the client's immediate experience.

> From the Handbook 2010

Experiments 2nd Essay

The method is designed to lead clients towards greater consciousness of the implicit beliefs that organize their reactions and experiences. That kind of information is not readily available to consciousness. What we do in Hakomi is create experiments using our guesses about what the unconscious material might be. We get our guesses from behaviors that are the surface expressions of those deep structures. We call them indicators. Good experiments almost always evoke the memories, images and beliefs that exist at the deeper levels. In order to make conscious what was unconscious (and to satisfy our curiosity by being detectives and scientists), we think, we guess and we experiment. All our techniques serve that end.

The discoveries that clients make are the outcomes of experiments. It's what this method does that other methods don't do. This is the only method I know of that does experiments in mindfulness. These experiments create moments of insight, you could say, assisted insight. Here's the sequence:

1. Once our relationship with the client is in place and the client understands what we're doing, we study the client for indicators and make our guesses about what they might mean and/or what experiment we might do to both test our guesses and possibly bring unconscious material into the client's consciousness.
2. We set the experiment up carefully: we prepare the client; we help the client become mindful; we explain what we're going to do.
3. We wait for the right moment and when everything's ready, we carefully do the experiment.
4. Then we watch for and/or ask for the outcome: the client's immediate reaction.

The process starts with loving presence and loving presence is maintained throughout. Still, you have to switch gears at some point so that you're doing two things at once. You're in loving presence - that should be an habitual state of mind that shapes all your behavior (your pace, your tone of voice, the way you look at people). At the same time, another habitual part of you is looking for indicators. You're also listening for key words and phrases. You're thinking about the client's belief system and childhood. All this is going on in the early phases of a session. Loving presence, however is the priority. Some part of you has to maintain loving presence even while you're doing all this gathering of information. You need information... so you can experiment!

Given that loving presence has been established, you search for indicators. When you find one, you create an experiment using it. You have to have the idea that the indicator is one that will probably lead to deeper material. You have to imagine what kind of experiments you could do with that indicator and maybe even what reactions they might lead to. Your experience with the method over time will help you do that. You do all this in your mind because you have to know what you're going to do. Since therapy is a real time process, you want to do this part rather quickly. Don't start to set up an experiment before you know what you're going to do. Experiments have to be set up in certain precise ways.

Here's what I mean: There are three essential parts of the set-up.

The first is: you describe the experiment to the client. You give clear instructions. You say something like, "I would like to do an experiment where you go into mindfulness and I will...blah, blah, blah." If it's going to be a probe, you might say something like, "In this experiment, you'll become mindful and when you're ready, you give me a signal and I'll make a statement and we'll notice what happens. Okay?" It helps clients relax a little when they have an idea about what the experiment is going to be like. You don't tell them what your statement is going to be—though you could do that and I have done it, without losing the power of the experiment. So, you give them a clear idea of what's expected of them and what you're going to do.

Experiments

After describing what you're going to do, you get permission to do it. "Is that okay with you?" Track for whether it really does seem okay. A client may say okay when they're really afraid or want to do something else. If you get clear, sincere permission, then you ask for and wait for mindfulness. You say, "Please become mindful and give me a signal when you're ready!" You track for signs that the client actually went into a mindful state. Watch for the signs of mindfulness and wait for the signal. The signs are: (1) the client becomes very still and (2) his or her eyelids flutter up and down over closed eyes. This movement of the eyelids is almost always an accurate sign that the client is in mindfulness. I use it all the time.

Of course, mindfulness is a radical shift in the way we pay attention. If you're working with a new client, you may have to teach him or her about what mindfulness is and you may have to help them get into it the first time.

Then, you do the experiment. If it's an effective experiment, you're going to get results. You're going to get useful outcomes. There are two kinds of useful outcomes: (1) there are emotional outcomes and there are (2) insight outcomes. Sometimes these are combined. If the emotions are intense, your path is to offer and provide comfort, if it's accepted. Maybe you take over some of the spontaneous management behaviors, if they allow that. You offer to support the client's spontaneous changes in posture and tensions. These are ways in which the adaptive unconscious attempts to manage strong emotional experiences. Whatever the client is doing to manage his or her emotions, you support that. For instance, if the client covers her face with her hands, you can have an assistant put her hands over the client's. That's if the emotion is intense.

If it's a mild emotion, you can still get reports about the experience or set up a second experiment based on the emotional reaction that occurred. When a client becomes sad after an experiment, or anytime during a session, I offer to have an assistant sit by the client or put an arm around her or a hand on her. If that is accepted, I sit silently and give the client time to feel the emotion and allow associations to arise. This very often leads to memories and/or insights. If it's an insight, if the client is quiet and you can see from her facial expressions that she is having thoughts and realizations, then just be silent and watch. I learned to do that late in my career. When the client is having insights, the best thing to do is to do nothing. Don't interfere! There's nothing you have to do. Insight is a very legitimate outcome of a good experiment. Just wait! You'll notice when the client is ready to interact again; he or she will come back into contact with you. Then you can say something like, "Had some insights, huh." Or, just look quietly at the client and she will probably tell you all about it.

We provide comfort and we provide silence in support of emotional reactions and insights.

Now, it doesn't always go that smoothly. Sometimes there's no reaction to an experiment.

Sometimes, the client has an immediate thought or an image or a memory. You have to know what to do with those things. With a thought, you might have an assistant take it over. That kind of taking over is a follow up experiment. Set it up the same way. There are experiments you can do with images and memories, also. Sometimes an experiment will evoke a child state of consciousness. Sometimes strong memories arise. There are ways to work with all of these. I won't go into the details on that now.

I want to emphasize two things about experiments. One is that they're central to the process and they require a certain precise care when you do them.

You can create experiments not only from physical indicators but also from deductions about what the client is saying or doing. For example, a client may have insights and not share them with you. That's a kind of indicator. You can think about things like that by asking yourself, "When does someone create a habit of not sharing?" "What kind of childhood did the person have?" "Why not share?" "What kind of belief system is behind that kind of behavior?" You do some of that kind of thinking. We can speculate that the person who doesn't share probably doesn't expect any help from others. It's one hypothesis we could have. So, we can then test that idea. Experiments are first of all tests of ideas. That they're evocative is part of it for our kind of work, but basically they are ways to testing your ideas about the client.

Experiments

> *"The test of all knowledge is experiment. Experiment is the sole judge of scientific 'truth.'"*
> (Feynman, 1964)

> *"In general, we look for a new law by the following process: First we guess it; then we compute the consequences of the guess to see what would be implied if this law that we guessed is right; then we compare the result of the computation to nature, with experiment or experience, compare it directly with observation, to see if it works. If it disagrees with experiment, it is wrong. In that simple statement is the key to science. It does not make any difference how beautiful your guess is, it does not make any difference how smart you are, who made the guess, or what his name is— if it disagrees with experiment, it is wrong."* (Feynman, 1964)

You set up experiments to test your ideas about the client. And the experiments you set up are also designed to evoke something. The reactions evoked give you answers to your questions and, if the experiments are good ones, they move the process towards insight and change. If you think not sharing is the result of a core belief that says, "don't expect help", then you do a probe like, "I'll help you." Or, you ask the client to fall backwards without looking back and you catch them. If falling back is difficult for the client or if saying "I'll help you" triggers crying and sadness, then you've tested your idea and you've moved the process.

I have one more very important thing to say about experiments. When you do an experiment, be sure to get the data. Get the data! Get the results! You're asking the client to, "Please notice your immediate reaction when...." You want to know what happened. If you can't see and hear what happened, get a report! That's one reason you did the experiment. To find out what would happen. You're not just curious, you also need that information to move the process. Of course, many times you will have noticed what happened. In that case, you don't have to ask for the data; you've already got it. Make a contact statement or something!

Well, what if they don't tell you their immediate reaction? What if they get dreamy and start saying something like, "You know, my mother used to make these cookies." Do you want to hear about cookies or do you want to know what the client experienced when you did the experiment? You're not there to listen to stories. An experiment can lead to diversions. If it seems to be doing that, interrupt. When you get a chance say, "So, you're remembering those great cookies, eh. I get that they tasted really good. But, you didn't tell me what happened with the experiment. Can you tell me that?" Get the data!

To summarize: by noticing indicators and making deductions, you get ideas about the client.

Then, you test those ideas by doing experiments. So, it's get ideas and test. Get ideas and test.

That's the information gathering operation within the therapy process. Experiments often evoke strong emotions and insights. That's another good thing that can happen. When it does happen, you follow through by working with the management of the emotion. All of this leads to discoveries. The process works when the client discovers something about his or her deepest convictions and models of the world. Because we're looking for that same information, we're leading the client to exactly what they need to get for themselves.

So, do experiments and get the data. The data can lead you to the next step in the process.

What you do next depends on what was evoked. That's also going to tell you whether your ideas are right or not. If you really wanted to practice the one thing that will give you the hang of the method, it's this: get ideas and test them. You'll not only be doing therapy, you'll be doing science. It's also fun. It's why people go hiking in the woods. It's why people read detective stories. It's why scientists stay up at night.

A transcript from a talk given to students in Tokyo in 2001

Taking Over

Taking over is one of the two or three most important techniques the method has. The use of mindfulness as it's done in Hakomi is certainly unique. But, while mindfulness, which is borrowed from spiritual practice, is always used in Hakomi in much the same way, techniques like taking over are specific in their application and different every time. These "little experiment" techniques, such as taking over and probes, are immensely inventive; they make the work very powerful and creative in the hands of a good "experimentalist". So, I want to describe a little bit about why taking over is so powerful.

As I reported in my book Body Centered Psychotherapy (Kurtz, 1990), taking over evolved out of something that happened during a workshop I gave over twenty years ago. A woman in a therapy process was getting very close to some extremely painful memory. She was lying on her back and as she came closer and closer to remembering this thing, she arched up off the floor, supporting herself on her heels and the back of her head. I felt so badly watching her that I decided to help her. I put my hand underneath her back and offered to take the weight of her body. When she relaxed and let me do that, the experience that she was keeping outside her consciousness immediately flooded her whole being. It came up as soon as she relaxed. Instead of feeling fear and anxiety, which she had just been experiencing—feelings that were being managed by the involuntary arching of her back—she now experienced only an overwhelming sadness. This sudden transition was a great surprise to me (and I think to her). It surprised me how easily the feared experience could be brought into consciousness, just by helping a person manage her avoidance of that experience.

Experiments

Later on, I associated this technique with one of the basic things Feldenkrais did in his work. To understand taking over, it will help to understand what Feldenkrais did and why he did it. Feldenkrais would take the weight of whatever part of the body he was working with. He would move it for the person. He wanted to teach people to move more effectively, with less effort. He would work with some people who couldn't move properly, like people with palsy, or who, for one reason or another, couldn't move an arm or a leg at all. He wanted to show how to move and how to move as easily as possible. As part of that teaching, he took the weight of the arm and made the movement for the person, over and over again, the same small movement, maybe fifty times. If the person couldn't extend her arm in a smooth way, if her arms shook so much she couldn't reach out for a glass of water and drink it without spilling it all, he would teach her how to do it. He takes all the little movements that are needed and he does each little movement with her hands, her wrists, her forearms. Each one, fifty times. As he does this, he watches the person's breathing. At some point the person relaxes and the breath becomes freer. This is the point where the person can feel the movement. It can sometimes take ten or fifteen minutes for that. But, when the person can feel the movement, they can also make the movement. Once something is experienced, the mind can find a way to recreate it. After all, whatever you experience is already something that the mind has created. How else could it have happened?

A big part of the problems with movement, even for ordinary people, is this: when they try to move, for example to turn their heads, they use more effort and more muscles than are needed. They try too hard. And, they haven't learned to use only the muscles that are needed. As a result, they are more tense than they need to be and that tension makes it hard for them to feel what an easier movement would feel like. For example, a person turning to see something might move his torso and shoulders and head and neck as if they were an indivisible unit. To remedy this, Feldenkrais moved each part by itself, so that the person could learn to differentiate one part from another. When they had learned that, the person could then move only the parts that are actually needed to do what he is trying to do. He gets the person to feel what

Experiments

that minimal effort/maximally efficient movement is like. And he does it by doing it for the person, over and over, until the person gets it. *"You can't do what you want till you know what you're doing"*, he used to say.

He takes the weight because he wants you to give up the tension. He does the movement for you, because he doesn't want you to effort. It is the tension that makes it difficult to feel. That's why the woman arched as she did. Some part of her mind, by creating this arching, had produced an enormous amount of tension in her body.... so she wouldn't feel the sadness. The arching was involuntary, as far as her conscious mind was concerned. It felt to her as if it was "just happening". But at some place outside of consciousness, it was of course deliberate. The point is—and it's not news—tension blocks feelings.

Here is an example. Some people believe, without being conscious of their belief, that they have to do everything for themselves, that no one will help them. This makes many ordinary things look much more difficult than they really are. People with such beliefs and perceptions become tense with the determination to succeed in spite of their isolation. The bodily expression of this determination is a mobilization of the muscles of the eyes, jaw, neck, shoulders and chest and legs, which says in effect, "I am ready to face life's challenges alone". This use of their body helps them to keep their loneliness and weakness out of consciousness, when these feelings threaten to emerge.

So, when we offer to take the weight of the shoulders and if the person gives us some of that weight, a moment later she feels the sadness that was waiting and right after that, a memory of being left alone comes into consciousness. This is the power of taking over.

This is a general pattern: tensions are used to manage painful experiences. When a person is managing painful experiences this way, at some level she believes she must do that. And this belief and the tensions it controls are habits. The woman had to arch the way she did. To her conscious mind, it just happened. So, when I offer to help her I'm offering this help to a part of her mind that believes it needs to manage the experience. I'm offering to be an ally to this part. I'm not trying to break through her "defenses" or to take anything away; I'm recognized as someone there to help. Something deep inside her recognizes that I'm on her side. This is another important part of taking over: the therapist is perceived to be an ally by the parts of the mind that manage painful experiences.

A prevalent way to think about management behavior is as "resistance". A therapist who challenges the resistance might, if a woman arched up as the woman above did, push down on her until she collapsed. If the therapist did that, it might very well have the effect of evoking contained sadness and hidden memories. It would work, so to speak. But it would also have the effect of turning the therapist into an enemy of those parts of the person trying to manage that experience. It would feel like the experiences were being forced out; that they were involuntary. The therapist would not feel like an ally. And the likely, long-term result would be a lot more "resistance" which, in my mind, would be justified and inevitable.

"It's like speeding up in a car when you're lost; the result usually just enables you to get lost over a wider area." (Penzias, 1989)

There are a different forms of taking over, both physical and verbal. All of them have the quality of supporting the client's emotional management behavior. They all carry the message: I'm on your side, I'll help you do whatever you believe you have to do to protect yourself, even if those beliefs themselves are not conscious. This makes an ally of the unconscious and, for a therapist, there is no more powerful ally than the client's unconscious. When I offer to take something over, the person doesn't have to allow that, she doesn't have to give me the weight, if she doesn't want to. There are people who can't give up the weight up their shoulders. They don't trust that much. That's another advantage of taking over: it's voluntary! The person proceeds at her own pace. People go deeper into themselves when they're ready. There's no sense of being forced. The method is nonviolent.

Experiments

Here's one more example. There are people who tighten the backs of their necks to keep from feeling hopeless. When I practiced bioenergetic approach myself, I would ask such a person to lie on a couch facing down with his head out over the end of the couch. Then I would push on the person's head until their neck muscles gave out, at which point they felt their hopelessness. Nowadays, I put such a person in same position and then, with my hands on the person's forehead, I offer to take the weight of the person's head. If the person accepts my offer, he can now practice, little by little, relaxing the neck muscles without collapsing or completely holding back. While I have the weight of their head, the person can experiment with feeling his hopelessness. That's the essence of taking over. To support a person's management behavior so that he can at his own pace, voluntarily relax it.

In the same way, we take over the reactions someone has to a statement given as a probe. Those spontaneous thoughts are very often also a form of management. When you take that over, it has the same effect as taking over any management behavior. The person voluntarily lets another person be that voice in order to allow himself to bring the hidden emotions, beliefs and memories that, without our ever knowing them directly, run those parts of ourselves we have not faced before.

Taking over is a way to offer a person a chance to relax, to give up some effort. Even when you are taking over a thought, by having someone else vocalize the thought, that's relieving tension. More accurately, it is the parts that operate from an involuntary place that give up the effort (if they wish to). When that happens, the person often begins to feel what was hidden from consciousness, like a painful memory or a dangerous impulse. So when we take something over, what very often happens is an emotion or image comes quickly and easily into consciousness and an emotional process is initiated.

For all these reasons, taking over is a powerful, nonviolent, creative set of techniques and a great part of what makes Hakomi the method that it is.

Healing & Missing Experiences

This chapter contains a series of essays taken from Ron's 2010 Training Handbook, 2010 Readings in the Hakomi Method, transcripts of talks to students, and an email commentary from Donna Martin on missing experiences. Together they provide students with Ron's breadth of thinking on the subject of healing and wholeness.

> A talk given to students in 2008, originally published in the Readings 2010

The Healing Process

The impulse to heal is real and powerful and lies within the client. Our job is to evoke that healing power, to meet its tests and needs and to support it in its expression and development. We are not the healers. We are the context in which healing is inspired.

Healing is a spontaneous process. It is genetically programmed and waiting to come online when needed. That's the way Stephen Porges describes the social engagement system. It's waiting to come online. In people who are autistic, it doesn't come online. It's available but, for some reason, it doesn't happen. The normal stimuli that would bring the social engagement system online don't do it.

Healing is another process that comes online spontaneously when you need it. A good example would be a cut finger. A cut finger repairs itself. You don't have to control that. If nothing interferes with the process and your body has the resources, it will heal itself. However, under certain conditions, the healing process, just like the social engagement system, doesn't come online.

Our concern is with the damage that has been done to a client's mental and emotional health. These systems can also be overwhelmed. When they are, they are handled by adaptations that work to prevent further damage, like becoming hyper-vigilant or going numb. Some adaptations interrupt or prevent the natural healing process. The damage cannot be integrated. The painful issue doesn't resolve. It gets shunted off to the side and stays there backstage. Repressed, it saps strength and energy, undermines clarity and in many ways, disturbs thinking, feeling and behavior. Sometimes it doesn't even stay backstage as when traumatic events are relived in flashbacks. Adaptations are in operation all the time. They are the myriad habits that are our everyday behavior. They're automatic and normally operate outside of consciousness.

Healing & Missing Experiences

So that's the first thing: healing is a spontaneous process that can get interrupted. Some psychotherapeutic techniques do exactly that; they interrupt the healing process, often when it is just beginning to happen. For example, something comes up in a therapy session and the client suddenly becomes sad. Some therapists are trained to ask things like: "Where do you feel that in your body?" Or, even worse, "Why are you sad?" The very act of asking questions too soon or too often interrupts the healing process. Anything that takes the client out of his experience and asks for information or an explanation, interrupts the natural emotional healing process. The client may not have the explanation. The process may just be beginning to unfold. It may be the start of a whole series of healing events being organized by the adaptive unconscious. It may just need time. It may need the therapist to remain silent. It is spontaneous. It will arise spontaneously and continue spontaneously, if it is not interrupted. For example, after the emotion has arisen, given time, memories and images may follow.

All you have to do when a healing process is underway is support it. You can often support the process, when sadness is the feeling, by a gentle touch on the arm or hand. Of course, touching is problematic for professional therapists. For ordinary people, and even some of our mammalian cousins, it's the obvious thing.

If you want to help, you don't ask questions and you don't make a lot of statements. You put a comforting hand on the person, stay silent, and wait. The client will probably close her eyes and deepen into her experience. She'll likely get memories and insights that will help integrate the original painful experience. This happens because, when you have a spontaneous emotion, the mind will automatically try to make sense of it and it will search for associations, ideas, beliefs, memories, and images that are coherent. But only if you do not interrupt.

The client may interrupt the process himself. That's what's been happening all along. If you have established a relationship in which the client knows, without thinking about it, that you will not interrupt, if you wait when the person stops to think, if you can wait when the client closes her eyes, if you can read the signs that the client is thinking or feeling something, concentrating on her own thoughts, memories and feelings, and just wait, you will be supporting the healing process. At some point the client will open her eyes and look at you. When she does, be there waiting. Let the client speak first. She will realize you have stayed connected. The client will have an unconscious sense that she can take her time, can go inside and begin to make sense of what's been happening to her. It may not make total sense immediately, but the process will be moving forward. The little things that come up when clients open their eyes and tell you what they've been experiencing are very important. What they tell you will most likely be something that will help the healing process continue.

So, that's how to help a healing process move towards completion. That's how you get to the memories and beliefs that are held in check by the adaptations that, while they offer affective protection, also prevent the healing. For me, the most important thing you can do is to learn to read the external signs that the person is doing internal work. They're not just sleeping in there, not just relaxed. They are processing. And there are signs that they're working, that their minds are working. The fact that they're not talking to you is perfect. You don't need an explanation. You don't need to know the story. You need to be able to wait patiently while the client does her inner work. When they come out, there may be something else to do, another step in the process. It may deepen at that point. Eventually, they come to an important, healing insight. The insight usually contains information about what was missing. Part of that missing experience is almost always somebody to do what you are doing right then. If you are comforting the person, or if you're waiting patiently, if you are listening, if you are sympathetic — those things could easily have been what was missing. Had it been there, the process might have completed already. It may complete now when all the right elements are in place. It's that simple.

From the Readings 2010

The Healing Relationship

I used to think of psychotherapy as intrapsychic, that the client did all the work internally. The therapist suggested things, but was, basically not really involved as a person. That was the way I thought. I thought of myself as a technician. My image was the samurai, in the movie Seven Samurais, who was a master swordsman, but who did what he did without emotions, passion or personality. His goal was perfect precision. I thought of myself in that same way, as trying to master techniques. It was no doubt inspired by a character flaw of mine, but I liked that image: precise, technical, without feelings or personal involvement. I took a secret pride in that.

Eventually though I saw that the difficulties that emerged in therapy were the result of my personal limitations, my incomplete personhood. They weren't technical problems at all and it wasn't about mastery. It was my ego, my puffed up attitude and my inability to understand people, because I didn't understand certain things in myself. It was about my ability to relate.

Again, the focus changed and the change was a vertical one. It was deeper than just technique. I came to a place where I focused for a few years on what I called the healing relationship. For a healing relationship to happen, more than just safety was needed; what was needed was the cooperation of the unconscious. It required a relationship at the level of the unconscious, a deep, person-to-person connection – and that's a two way street. Not only did I learn that I needed the cooperation of the unconscious, I also learned that I had to be worthy of it. I needed to earn it.

The healing relationship involves two basic things. First, the therapist has to demonstrate that she's trustworthy, non-judgmental and compassionate. Second, she has to demonstrate that she is present, attentive and really understands what's going on for the person. If the therapist can consistently demonstrate those things to the person, she will earn the cooperation of the unconscious.

The unconscious is waiting for somebody who can do that. If the client has painful secrets, shame, confusion and emotional pain, the therapist will need extraordinary sensitivity, understanding and caring to become an ally of the unconscious. The unconscious has been managing this pain for a long time. It won't allow just anyone to become part of that process. The healing relationship is about gaining the trust and cooperation of the unconscious through compassion and understanding. If you can do that, therapy really happens. Building such a relationship doesn't have to take three months or three years. It can take as little as fifteen minutes. But creating it requires more than just technical skills.

The creation of a healing relationship in therapy requires that the therapist be a certain kind of person, a person who is naturally compassionate, able to be radically present, able to give full attention to another, able to see deeply into people and to understand what is seen. All of that takes a certain state of mind. We could call that state of mind non-egocentric. The therapist needs to be free of as many ego-centered habits as possible when working with the client. Realizing that and teaching that was the next big vertical jump for Hakomi. This jump was beyond just the use mindfulness and non-violence. It was about who the therapist was, the therapist's being. It was about the therapist's consciousness.

From the Readings 2010

The Right State of Mind

When I realized the importance of the client-therapist relationship, I began to understand something about "the other as a true interiority". I call what we do at this level of the work, developing the healing relationship. I believe very strongly in the power of the unconscious mind. I agree with Jung (as cited in Hall and Nordby, 1973) about its enormous capabilities and its connection to what John Nelson called the "Spiritual Ground" (Nelson, 1994). It seems to me that in order to work successfully, we have to have the cooperation of the client's adaptive unconscious. For that we need to demonstrate two things. First, we need to demonstrate that we know what's going on, particularly that we understand the person's present experience. Second, we have to demonstrate that we are compassionate and caring. We must not be judgmental. If we can demonstrate those two things, the adaptive unconscious will almost always cooperate. Not that it will give you anything you want, no. But, if you maintain your good behavior, it will allow you to be part of the healing process. It will listen to you and take you seriously. It will return the respect you show it. Most importantly, it will allow the process to unfold and it will "lead the way" with what is for the client spontaneous impulses and memories.

Understanding and compassion are not techniques. To create a healing relationship, they must be real. You can't just say you understand or just look compassionate. That won't fool anyone's unconscious for very long. You've got to really be compassionate. When you do understand and when you are compassionate and can successfully demonstrate that you are, then you'll get the cooperation of the unconscious. Then the work will progress smoothly, easily and faster. The unconscious can unfold healing in most remarkable ways.

When the context is right, the work will go well. If the therapist does not create the right context, the process will take a long time.

Healing & Missing Experiences

That satisfied me for a while, this work with the healing relationship. I have come to realize that the work I have to do to become a full human being involves creating the right state of mind. With the right state of mind, understanding and compassion come quite naturally, without effort, the healing relationship is developed without effort, the method and techniques work easily and the process moves more quickly.

From the Readings 2010

Stewardship

Martha Herbert (2000) has a paper on stewardship that names two contrasting world views or systems of belief. The first worldview she calls a control-oriented disconnected belief system; the second, a stewardship-oriented connected belief system.

Two belief systems. Two world views. One about control. One about stewardship. Both with related assumptions and elaborate implications for the way we live and work in this world, implications about who we are and how we relate to one another and the environment. I'd like to talk about these systems of belief in relation to the Hakomi Method.

One of the great teachings of Taoist philosophy is that nature works best when it is not interfered with. "Spring comes and the grass grows by itself" is an old Zen saying. Nowadays, there's much talk about self-organizing systems. You could say, spring comes and the grass self-organizes. Not very good as poetry, but the message is basically the same. That is, there are forces at work that do not need human control. The brain, it has been estimated, utilizes two billion bits of information per second, only two thousand of which are used by the conscious mind. There's a lot going on without our control, even without our awareness. Several recent papers and books attest to this.

Healing & Missing Experiences

Some other, much greater intelligence is organizing all that. Imagine you had to control all the chemical reactions taking place in your body and all the nervous processing taking place in your brain. Not even possible to imagine.

The healing processes often work just fine with a minimum of control-oriented disconnected belief system interference. Nourishment and rest work well for the body and much the same will work for the mind.

Consider this, Pierre Janet, the great French psychologist (as cited in Bargh and Chartrand,1999), believed that psychological illness was brought about this way: At a point in time when a person is emotionally vulnerable, an upsetting incident can overwhelm the mind. The person does not have the resources to integrate the event in a way that makes sense and can be incorporated into their knowledge of the world. The event is somehow contained and the integration process fails to happen, leaving the person with an encapsulated emotional event, buried in the unconscious. Although this buried event remains outside of consciousness and unintegrated, it creates an irritation of a sort and affects the person's mental states and behavior. Among the effects are the development of habits and beliefs, and unconscious behaviors that control feelings and memory and keep the unintegrated material from reaching consciousness.

Conditions needed for healing and integration dictate the three broad phases of the method. First, we must create a relationship within which the painful work can be done. Second, we must bring the unintegrated event into consciousness. And third, we must support the process of integration. For bringing material habitually kept out of consciousness, we must have permission, cooperation and an effective method. There are ways to overwhelm the defenses and bring such events into consciousness, but these ways can have negative effects. They may re-create the traumatic experience (Bromberg, 2006).

A forceful approach automatically elicits resistance and a great expenditure of energy. Force is neither sensible nor effective for most healing. Think of a cut finger! Or growing roses. Yes, we can support these processes, but forcing them is not even possible. Not to mention the pain and resistance that attempting to control them may cause.

However, such processes can be stewarded. In this method the evocation of the unconscious event is done with the conscious knowledge and spoken permission of the client. Clients understand that the experiments that are set up are designed to evoke emotions and memories of such events. An experiment done well will often start a healing process and clients know this. Clients are somewhat prepared when they go into mindfulness. They can control their reactions to some extent.

When intense and painful emotions arise, the stewardship of the healing process begins. Such processes are spontaneous and there are clear ways to steward it. Doing so requires kindness, containment and possibly comforting touch. It especially requires sensitivity and recognition of the need for silence during the moments when the client is integrating. These things "nourish" the process. When the grass grows by itself, it still needs good soil, a little rain and some sunshine.

The Natural Course of Healing

> *"In this perspective individual behaviors that are usually seen as symptomatic of personal ill health can be seen as functional, adaptive, and useful for the individual in the system within which he operates. Although they boomerang on the actor in ways she does not like, they testify to her basic strength and resourcefulness, wiliness even, rather than her weakness." (Joanna Macy, 1991)*

I don't think of the Refined Hakomi Method as curing disease. I think of it as a specific type of learning, the unlearning of adaptations that cause unnecessary suffering. I think that way because, as with all aspects of human development, adjustments have to be made based on experience.

Healing, in general, is an inner-directed process. Early in the development of Hakomi, I stated this quite clearly when I wrote "The answer is within," meaning, within the client. I have also written, "The impulse to heal is real and powerful and lies within the client. Our job is to evoke that healing power, to meet its tests and needs and to support it in its expression and development."

We are not the healers. We are the context in which healing is inspired.

Mental-emotional healing is "coordinated and controlled" by the adaptive unconscious. Often, our experiments done with the client in mindfulness, initiate a healing process. This is marked by spontaneous thoughts and memories and/or the sudden experience of an emotion. We support the healing process in several ways. When the client becomes sad, we offer a gentle physical contact, when the client goes inside and shows external signs of processing—like eyes closed, little nods, quick changes in facial expression—we remain silent. This is because an emotion will draw associations to it, like memories and thoughts that help explain the presence of the emotion.

When spontaneous management behaviors arise, we support them if we have permission to do so. In Hakomi terms, this is "taking over". We pay particular attention to the emergence of spontaneous events, like impulses, memories, thoughts and emotions. These are often clues to the direction the process should take and are signs of the operations of the adaptive unconscious. When such events occur, we try to utilize them in what we do next, like another experiment. This aspect of the process is called following.

Mental-emotion healing processes often start after an experiment in mindfulness. There are spontaneous processes that will unfold given the right conditions; as best we can, we provide those conditions. The best conditions for healing are loving presence of the therapist, non-interference with the process, gentle touch, holding and comforting, and attention, silence and patience.

As part of the natural course of a healing process, memories and thoughts that make sense of the emotional reaction are drawn into consciousness that help make sense of it. And that's exactly what we want to have happen!

During this process, we track for the external signs that the client is having memories and insights and is integrating the emotional experience, signs of deep concentration on the face and nods of the head, indicating realization or agreement with some idea.

During this process, the client is gathering memories and ideas and is making sense of them, making sense of what just happened and what happened long ago that left confusion, that left painful feelings unfinished and without meaning or coherence.

After an experiment in mindfulness, clients often start doing this internal work. While doing this, they often have a precise memory that makes sense of their reactions and they may be able to articulate the implicit beliefs it created.

The process may cycle through emotions, associations, insights, memories, deeper emotions, more associations, and so forth.

Missing Experiences

Certain powerful formative experiences required painful but necessary adaptations and for some of these experiences, the elements that might have promoted healing were missing. Some experiences are difficult to integrate and aspects of those unintegrated experiences express themselves through habits and implicit beliefs that help manage the difficulties they are still causing. These habits are functions of the adaptive unconscious.

Sometimes there is one fundamental missing experience: the presence of someone calm, sympathetic, patient and understanding to care for the suffering person and support the healing process. Beyond this fundamental missing experience, there are a great variety of other healing experiences that can be created for the client.

When we help bring a limiting core belief into consciousness, we then want to provide an experience that challenges it. Some core beliefs are extreme and rigidly maintained. For example, a person might believe, at a core level, that no one can be trusted. A devastating experience of betrayal can make this belief seem to be a good one to hold, since it protects against further betrayal. A person with this core belief will be cautious with everyone and won't really trust anyone. This person may withdraw from contact and prefer to be alone – because it feels safer. Well, this model is extremely limiting. The truth is that some people are trustworthy and some people aren't. Some people will hurt you and some people won't. You just have to be able to tell the difference. To do that, you will need to experience trust. It is a missing experience we now work to create.

You won't know the depth of your distrust until something happens to illuminate it. When you work with this issue, it may become clear that you've never felt safe anywhere. Now you can work with that fear, go through it, survive it, finish it, and create the possibility of feeling safe.

An important part of the method is creating a missing experience. It can be powerful. Someone who has never felt safe is going to have a powerful experience when they finally do. What's useful is to spend time with it, stabilizing it and creating access routes to it. Taking time with it feels quite natural to the client. Together, we basically just wait for each new insight and we study the many aspects of the experience. I don't lead this process. I follow it.

I want to give the client time to fully absorb it, memorize it, savor it, learn about it and try it on again and again. The important thing is to integrate it. The client may experience a series of emerging insights. I may simply watch, making an occasional agreeable comment. The client may speak about these insights or she may not. When this missing experience is savored and stabilized, the client changes. The old model is wrong now or at least incomplete. It has to be revised. A core model has enormous implications, on all levels, from physiology to relationship. It takes a long time to integrate. In a typical session, it might take thirty minutes to arrive at the missing experience and another twenty to thirty minutes to savor it. It might take years to fully integrate it.

In order to really stabilize the new model, the person has to use it, in all kinds of applicable situations. Changes like this are integrated, one decision at a time.

> From Integration and the Missing Experience, Readings 2010

What is Missing?

What kinds of experiences are missing and how missing are they? As to what kind of experiences are missing, the ones that are important to therapeutic practice are the ones involving the social emotions, experiences around relationship. That's what's missing. When I think about all the missing experiences I've helped evoke in clients, safety, contact, comfort, all the positive, nourishing experiences, they are all about relationship. Of course, they are all taking place within the relationship with the therapist and the group. That makes it part of the "social brain", the interaction between brains. This is, in Schore's much used term, "interactive psychobiological regulation." (Schore, 1994). The therapist and the group are providing the kind of sensitive, nourishing responses that give needed support for the development of a secure sense of self and social-emotional skills, the same exact support an infant needs from the parenting one and for the same reasons.

Another question to ask is how are these experiences missing? I've found two strong ways experiences become missing. One, there is fear that prevents the kinds of actions and/or organization that would allow the experience, like the fear that reaching out might bring rejection. By organization, I mean that perception and memory are organized to avoid, minimize or escape the consequences of seeking the missing experience. The missing experience is a positive one, which would normally be desired, but the personal history associated with that experience is painful. The offering of the missing experience in the therapeutic setting begins to evoke those painful memories and the habits that manage such situations take over. Fears of being hurt, disappointed, humiliated motivate avoidance of what is actually desirable.

Actions also avoid situations where the experience might occur. The fear is not always conscious and may be the first thing to be evoked when working with the issue.

Secondly, experiences are missing due to a kind of blindness, which we can call trance. The person just doesn't know about the experience. He can't see it. He can't remember it. He cannot attend to it, even when it is happening right in front of him. As part of the trance, there is also an imagined powerlessness. That is, the person has no sense that they are doing anything to keep the experience from happening (Wolinsky, 1991).

Donna Martin's email to Ron regarding missing experiences:

"I still see a way that some people tend to misunderstand when you talk about "evoking early memories"... as if we are evoking accurate memories of early events or situations... and somehow fixing things that happened or didn't happen in the past. It's a subtle point as I know that past experiences have shaped us and wounded us and are stored as "memories" in our habitual way of perceiving and making meaning of present events and therefore of reacting in present time. It's so easy, though, for therapists to get trapped in the idea that we are somehow healing someone's history. What I love about Hakomi is its focus on present experience - and experiencing - as the only valid place we can participate and therefore change things. It is useful to know that a person's beliefs and reactions are adaptations to past experiences... experiences being the key word as it may have to do with what happened or didn't happen, but it could also have to do with the way the child perceived and made meaning of what was happening... often/usually inaccurately. The truth is we can only guess about that, and I think that our guesses are somewhat irrelevant in terms of how we can support the person to open up to new possibilities. The more we even imply that we are there to repair damage or wounding that was done in the past, the more we are in danger of colluding with the idea that

something is wrong - blaming someone's history and becoming rescuers - rather than empowering people to wake up to the unnecessary suffering caused by their own habits and beliefs... whatever they were based on. Instead of "evoking early memories" would it be accurate to say that we are tracking for indicators of, and possibly evoking examples of the client's way of remembering as it shows us how the client is organizing present experience based on ideas and beliefs and perceptual and behavioral habits that are probably a result of past experiences which we can only guess at. I am intensely concerned with avoiding the psychotherapeutic tendency to pathologize and approach therapy in terms of what is (or was) wrong and needs to be righted, especially with the kind of clients that Hakomi works best for, who are capable of and willing to self-study and to open up to more of the available ways of being nourished by Life."

Integration

> *"Emotionally meaningful events can enable continued learning from experience throughout the lifespan. Such learning may be seen as, in effect, the ongoing development of the brain. Experience plays a primary role in stimulating new neuronal connections in both memory and developmental process."* (Siegel, 1999)

Missing experiences are experiential, relational, positive, and conducive to establishing a sense of coherence in an individual. Ordinarily, I talk about core beliefs influencing the organization of experience, but it's more than just beliefs. The functioning of an integrated mind includes not only beliefs, but attitudes, intentions, thoughts, feelings, images and memory.

The missing experience, no matter what the belief or situation that evokes it, is always a positive experience. It always provides relief or pleasure and a new, more positive sense of self. A missing experience occurs within a sensitive, highly attuned relationship with the therapist and in some cases, with a group.

The conditions of support for the missing experience seem clear enough. We have to be extremely sensitive to the other person's mental-emotional state and we have to adapt to it. That's what we call tracking and the adjustment to unconscious needs. We have to know what to do when people are in various mental states. Those states are often not conscious. That is, clients may not recognize or have words to describe and think about the state they are in. They may not have practiced self-observation in a serious way. It is as if they do not really know who they are and what their situation is. And, we must meet them there, where they are. So, we have to be present in a special way, sensitive, adaptive and very "with" the other person. Of course we also have to be compassionate and caring.

It may be that in order to support affect regulation in our clients, we therapists will have to cultivate a particular state of mind in ourselves, one that evokes a state of mind in our clients that the loving mother evokes in her infant. Neurologically speaking, one right hemisphere talking to another. We need to convey a calm, compassionate concern for the client. The state of mind that does best is the one sustained by a well developed ability to take pleasure in the success and happiness of the other. Call it compassion or sympathetic joy. Call it unconditional positive regard. Call it love. Call it what you will. It remains the prime responsibility of the therapist. Open-heartedness has a unique power to effect positive change. It's a sweet feeling too and good for one's own mental health. Just being in that state of mind where one is present and sensitive and able to respond to the client's emotional needs, does ninety percent of the work. The rest is the occasional technical intervention that moves the process along.

Integration occurs slowly as new, more realistic beliefs are formed. Energy is drained away from the long struggle and becomes available for living this very moment. Confusion yields to clarity. A delicious joy is felt and the pleasure of seeing new positive possibilities arises. In the process of integration, we witness the natural course of things.

For people who have suffered trauma and for therapists who work with trauma, I recommend the work of Pat Ogden (2006) and Peter Levine (1997).

Process & Structure

The following essays are compiled from the 2010 Training Handbook for the Refined Hakomi Method and the 2010 Readings in the Hakomi Method of Mindfulness-Based Assisted Self Study. Some of the pieces have been expanded from bullet to essay format in order to clarify Ron's teachings. Some of the pieces have remained in bullet form for conciseness and clarity. This section will help students understand the logic and process of the method.

An Outline of the Method

1. **Assisted Self Discovery**
   Seeing the work as assisted self discovery is one of the major differences between this refined method and the original Hakomi and other psychotherapies. A second major difference between Hakomi and other psychotherapies, one that is unique to Hakomi at the moment, is simply that we do precise experiments in mindfulness. The method of assisted self discovery requires not only the skills of the practitioner, it also requires explicit commitments on the part of the person being assisted.

2. **Qualities and skills required of a practitioner**
   Practitioners must be able to sustain a compassionate and present-centered state of mind, a state we call loving presence. Loving presence combines several habits of feeling, attention and mindset. It is an integrated combination of attitude, emotional state and focus of attention. Compassion is the first and most important element, being present is the second. To be continuously present is to continuously stay focused on the observable behaviors of the moment, especially the client's non-verbal activities that modulate communication and regulate the relationship. In particular, the therapist must observe the signs of the client's present experience and the client's general qualities and habitual behaviors and that kind of attention requires overcoming one of our strongest, most common habits, namely gathering information through questions and conversation. Practitioners must become masters of reading the information in nonverbal behaviors. Six skill sets are necessary for practitioners and are described later in this chapter.

3. **Commitments and skills required of the "client"**
   In Hakomi we use the term "the client", but no longer do we think about them in regular psychotherapeutic terms. Clients in the refined method may be thought of as self-studying, that is seeking after the truth of who one has become and how with help one may explore and resolve the issues that trouble and confine one. The

client must be capable of entering into a present-centered, experience-focused, non-controlling and vulnerable state of mind (mindfulness). She must understand that the process includes as a central element, experiments done in mindfulness. The client must be willing to enter into that process even though painful emotions may arise. These are the commitments and skills required of people who are clients in the refined method of Hakomi. If the person is very anxious or easily distracted, or is someone who does not understand what the process actually requires, then the work can be difficult or impossible without some prior preparation.

4. **Experiments**

Experiments are done with the client in a mindful state and are specifically designed to evoke reactions that will help bring unconscious material such as foundational memories, underlying emotions and implicit beliefs into consciousness. Reactions to experiments are noticed in mindfulness and reported to the therapist. Reactions can be thoughts, feelings, images, impulses, memories, tensions or any combination of these. The result of the experiments are the data from which we design subsequent experiments in an iterative process of self exploration.

5. **Nonverbal Behaviors**

There are two kind of nonverbal behaviors that are of primary interest: the external signs of the client's present experience and observable indicators of core material. Noticing the momentary ones is one of the ways we build and maintain our relationship with the client. Noticing the habitual ones gives us clues to the memories, emotions and implicit beliefs that organize what the client can and cannot experience and is an important step in setting up and doing experiments. Habits are often expressions of adaptations to powerful formative events and may point toward important, underlying issues that control the client's behavior.

6. Nonverbal Awareness: Tracking

Tracking is the ability to gather two kinds of nonverbal information, signs of the client's present experience and indicators of core material. Tracking is noticing what the client is doing and experiencing, moment by moment. It is an essential part of being present. We use the information gained by tracking to connect with and to stay connected with the client, by making contact statements. A contact statement names the client's present experience, quickly and simply. Tracking and contact are two basic techniques in the original Hakomi method.

7. Nonverbal Awareness: Indicators

Practitioners train themselves to notice behaviors that could be indicators of core material. These are certain personal qualities and habitual behaviors of clients, such as postures, gestures, facial expressions, tones of voice and speech patterns. A few simple examples of indicators are: habitually shrugging ones shoulders, tilting one's head, interrupting ones own speech, or speaking very quickly. The expression left on a relaxed face is a prime indicator. Habits like these are designed to operate automatically, without conscious attention. Habits like these allow consciousness to be preserved for the non-routine things that require fresh decisions. Indicators are one of the two main sources of experiments. The second source involves listening to statements for implications and assumptions. Knowing how to create an experiment using indicators is essential. The practice of searching for and using indicators has become a significant part of teaching and practicing the refined method.

8. Experiments and Their Effects

Experiments are done with the client in a mindful state. When a particular indicator has been noticed and chosen, the next step is to get an idea for an experiment. Once you have an idea, you ask the client to become mindful and to signal when they are ready. When the client signals that he or she is ready, you do the experiment. If you've chosen a good indicator, and if you've done a good experiment with it, you're likely to get a reaction that can begin the healing and discovery process for the client. The reaction may also suggest or bring into consciousness the core material associated with it. If the reaction is an emotional one, I do two things that weren't done in previous versions of the method: I touch the client (more likely, I have an assistant touch the client.) And secondly, I remain silent while the client turns inward and looks like she is doing inner work.

9. **About Using Touch**
Touching clients is normally not recommended for psychotherapists. This is primarily due to legal considerations. When I use touch, I first get permission and, since I use assistants and may have several other observers present, I feel quite comfortable using touch. Once permission has been established, assistants will generally touch without asking again. For a client who is experiencing sadness as a reaction to an experiment, a gentle touch signals the client that we are aware that he or she is emotional, and that we are sympathetic and paying attention. If there are signs that the client is working internally, (eyes closed, facial movements and nods of the head) we do not interrupt. We wait patiently for the client to open his or her eyes, look at us and speak. In these moments of silence, the client is integrating something, making sense of the feelings, memories and thoughts that arise in reaction to an experiment. Silence, accompanied by gentle touch, helps the client to stay with his or her experience.

10. **The Natural Course of a Healing Process**
Mastery of the world is achieved by letting things take their natural course.(Tao Te Ching)
Mental-emotion healing processes often start after an experiment in mindfulness. These are spontaneous processes that will unfold given the right conditions. As best we can, we provide those conditions. What are the conditions for healing? The process must not be interrupted or interfered with; gentle touch or holding and comforting when appropriate; attention, silence and patience. As

Process & Structure

part of the natural course of a healing process, memories and thoughts that make sense of the emotional reaction are drawn into consciousness, helping make sense of it. And that's exactly what we want to have happen!

During this process, we track for the external signs that the client is having memories and insights and is integrating the emotional experience, signs of deep concentration on the face and nods of the head, indicating realization or agreement with some idea.

During this process, the client is gathering memories and ideas and is making sense of them, making sense of what just happened and what happened long ago that left confusion, that left painful feelings unfinished and unsorted out.

After an experiment in mindfulness, clients often start doing this internal work. While doing this, they often have a precise memory that makes sense of their reactions and they may be able to articulate the implicit beliefs it created. The process may cycle through emotions, associations, insights, memories, deeper emotions, more associations, and so forth.

11. Missing Experiences

Certain powerful formative experiences required painful but necessary adaptations. For some of these experiences, the elements that might have promoted healing were missing. Janet says, they couldn't be made sense of and as a result, they didn't get integrated. They remained "an irritation" unconsciously affecting feelings and behavior in a negative way (Rossi, 1996). Some aspects of those unintegrated experiences express themselves through habits and implicit beliefs that help manage the difficulties they are still causing. These habits are functions of the adaptive unconscious. There is one fundamental missing experience: the presence of someone calm, sympathetic, patient and understanding to care for the suffering person and support the healing process. Beyond this fundamental missing experience, there are a great variety of other healing experiences that can be created for the client. During the healing process, the client often relives an old painful event.

Process & Structure

Quietly comforting the client is one of the main components of the missing experience.

12. Integration

Slowly, resolutions are accomplished; new, more realistic beliefs are formed. Energy is drained away from the long struggle and becomes available for living this very moment. Confusion yields to clarity. A delicious joy is felt and the pleasure of seeing new positive possibilities arises. This is the process of integration, the natural course of things.

Guidelines for the Way Things Work

Mutual Causality

> *"In this doctrine [the Dharma] everything arises through mutual conditioning in a reciprocal interaction. Indeed the very word Dharma conveys not a substance or essence, but orderly process itself—the way things work." (Macy, 1991)*

> *"A good therapist, shares control with everything present, sometimes moving deeply into the unfolding action, sometimes waiting quietly as the other does inner work, surfing gracefully the changing amplitudes of intimacy." (Kurtz)*

From the perspective of mutuality, our part in the client's process is basically to assist in the client's self-study. We do not need to see ourselves as directors of the process. When we don't, a new kind of relationship can emerge, one of mutual influences. Our respect for the healing power that lies within the client gives rise to the client feeling free to go inside and feel what's next for her. The client's sense of safety and freedom allows her to consider our suggestions and ideas without the need to defend against being manipulated. Her respect for our suggestions makes our adjustments to her spontaneous behaviors simple and generally successful.

Not a Lot, But Enough

> *"I always tell the students that it's easy to have a complicated idea, but it's very, very hard to have a simple idea. Often, that means thinking about them in new ways, that aren't just the way everybody else is thinking about them." (Mead)*

> *"The simplest way to achieve simplicity is through thoughtful reduction." (Gell-Mann, TED talks)*

> *"Make everything as simple as possible but not simpler." (Einstein)*

According to Occam's razor, all other things being equal, the simplest explanation is the most likely to be true. A description of the method can be made simple. However, as Mead points out, doing that is "very, very hard". He talks about thinking in new ways. That is certainly what I've attempted to do with my ideas about the method.

Given the complexities of human interactions and healing, what I've written below is the best I can do... So far.

The simplicity of the method isn't obvious to naïve witnesses. It resides in the learned behavior of the accomplished practitioner. Being simple doesn't mean it's not creative and flexible. On the contrary, simplicity is the source of its power and creativity. For example, when the harmonic structure of a piece of music is simple, the melody lends itself most easily to improvisation. When a player knows that structure completely, he can improvise. He need not think about it.

> *"Learn simple things first and learn them to perfection." (Kelley, 1994)*

It's the same with the process. When you ground yourself in the basics, no conscious thought is needed for its implementation. Learning the signs and steps that constitute the process and learning them to perfection is the beginning of excellence. Then, the work is easy, creativity becomes possible and brings delight, and consistent success.

Here are twelve essential elements of the process, good things to practice to perfection:

1. **Being and staying in loving presence**

2. **Tracking**, being continuously aware of the client's present experience
3. **Making contact statements**, short, non-invasive statements that name the client's present experience you've been tracking
4. **Watching for indicators**, habitual verbal and nonverbal expressions which could be expressions of implicit beliefs and adaptations
5. **Mentally modelling the client's mind** - mental modelling is what we're doing when we use external signs to get ideas about what the other person is feeling or thinking at the moment, or when we get ideas or make guesses about his or her history, adaptations and beliefs
6. **Helping to establish and supporting mindfulness** in the client
7. **Creating** and **doing experiments** using indicators and good guesses
8. **Studying and using the outcomes of experiments**
9. **Following**: using the client's spontaneous behavior to move the process forward
10. **Being silent** when the client needs time to be inside, e.g. when integration is happening.
11. **Supporting the client's healing process** by recognizing its emergence and the spontaneous integration which normally accompanies it and by providing comforting, periods of silence, and when needed, containment.
12. **Creating the missing** experience by providing opportunities for the client to experience the emotions and realizations that were not possible within the client's old beliefs and adaptations.

Here are some guidelines for the twelve elements:

Process & Structure

1. **Loving Presence**
    - search for something in the client that inspires warm feelings
    - avoid asking questions
    - avoid having an ordinary conversation
    - stay relaxed and stay focused on the aspects that inspire
    - allow your demeanor to be shaped by your warm feelings

2. **Tracking**
    - make a habit of constantly noticing signs of the client's present experience
    - be especially observant of when the client's experience changes
    - be especially observant of signs of emotions rising
    - watch the whole body
    - watch for gestures, facial expressions, shifts in posture, nervous movements
    - listen for attitudes expressed in the tone of voice
    - watch for gestures that can be seen as "unconscious comments" on what's being discussed. A simple example is a shrug of the shoulders.

3. **Contact Statements**
    - make them as short as possible - for example, "sad, huh?"
    - your tone should be such that it says, "I'm open to being corrected." That's what the "huh" is about. It's halfway between a statement and a question.
    - make a contact statement whenever the client's experience changes significantly
    - make a contact statement when you notice the first signs of an emotion arising
    - don't make a lot of contact statements, only enough to establish in the client's mind that you're generally aware of what she is experiencing. Too many can become annoying for the client.

- although you may occasionally contact the ideas the client is presenting, it's best not to do too much of this; it encourages thinking, explaining and storytelling

4. **Watching for Indicators**
    - indicators are habitual verbal and nonverbal outward expressions which could be outward expressions of adaptations and implicit beliefs
    - watch for these habitual behaviors, like the resting facial expression, or a repeated gesture
    - find the ones you already know about or those that seem most interesting to you
    - again, watch the whole body, especially habits of posture, facial expression, and tone of voice

5. **Modelling the Client's Mind**
    - from the indicators, make some guesses about what beliefs, implicit beliefs, adaptations to early situations, history, thinking—all the internal structuring that influences the client's experiences
    - possibly make a contact statement naming your guesses about your ideas
    - frame these guesses as sources for experiments
    - come up with an idea for an experiment
    - once you've picked an indicator to work with, ask the client if he or she is willing to do an experiment
    - if yes, set up an experiment

6. **Establishing Mindfulness**
    - generally, you only have to do this with a new client. When you've worked with someone for a while, the person should be able to go right into mindfulness when asked

Process & Structure

- you should speak in a slightly hypnotic way, softly and slowly emphasizing non-action and attention to the flow of present experience
- there are signs in the client's demeanor that indicate mindfulness - chief among these is the movement up and down of the eyeball under closed lids
- other signs are stillness, easy breathing, very relaxed look
- once mindfulness is established, set up and do the experiment

7. Doing the Experiment
- ask permission and set it up and if it needs explaining, describe the client's role
- use phrases like, "if you're ready" and "please notice" and "tell me what happens when..."
- do the experiment and ask for the outcome if it is not obvious or offered
- track for the outcome

8. Studying and using the outcomes of experiments
- there may be several possible directions to take, given different kinds of outcomes
- if the client seems confused, you might want to repeat the experiment
- if the reaction is obvious, make a contact statement
- if the client has his or her eyes closed, wait for the client to speak first
- if the reaction is sadness, have an assistant offer to put a hand on the client
- if there's no reaction, contact that and wait for the client to speak
- if the reaction is tension, do the tension sequence
- if the reaction is an impulse that's not executed, take over the holding back

- be inventive!

9. Following and using the client's spontaneous behaviors
- when something spontaneous arises for the client, especially if it is conscious and surprising to the client, find a way to use it in the next experiment
- consider these spontaneous behaviors as signals from the adaptive unconscious
- following is a general principle in moving the process forward. An example of following is making contact statements when the client's present experience is changing. In that case, after the contact statement, it's usually a good idea to wait to see what the client says and does, and use that to move forward.
- following requires a habit of often remaining silent and waiting to see what direction the client takes
- following implies having faith in the client's healing process

10. Being Silent when the client needs time to be inside
- an especially important time to be silent is when the client is integrating a new experience
- signs of integration are closed eyes, movements in the face that suggest internal dialogue
- nodding of the head is especially important as it signals understanding
- wait with your focus on the client when his or her eyes finally open
- silence creates spaciousness and signals the client that you will give her the time she needs to study her thoughts, memories and experiences, without your needing to interrupt or control her process.
- silence, like following, is a way to honor the client's healing process

Process & Structure

11. Supporting the Client's Healing Process

- recognize the emergence of healing and the spontaneous integration which normally accompanies it and provide comforting, periods of silence, and when needed, containment
- stay as calm and focused as you can and leave space by being silent when the client is processing emotions
- use touch - I have assistants touch and/or hold the client, usually without speaking
- containment, like taking over bodily contraction during the experience of fear, is another way to support the healing process
- if there is a strong sense in the client of a child-like state of mind being present, you can work directly with the accompanying feelings and memories. Do what any compassionate and skillful adult would do to help
- what might be needed is to be understood, to feel cared for, to offer time to recover and integrate, to make meaning of what might have happened
- sometimes soothing and calming sounds or words will help
- it is important to follow the client's spontaneous behaviors during the healing phase

12. Creating the Missing Experience

- we provide opportunities for the client to experience the emotions and realizations that were not possible within the client's old beliefs and adaptations
- as part of the healing process and integration, it may be useful to create an experience for the client that was not possible before the implicit beliefs, memories and adaptations became conscious;
- examples of missing experiences could be that someone is patient, paying attention, not being judgmental
- you can use assistants or a whole group if they're available to offer nourishing statements that were automatically

rejected before and are now accepted and have evoked good feelings
- sometimes it can be support for something the client does or says, like people smiling or clapping or joining in
- the criterion for success here is the enjoyment and pleasure the client feels when these things are done
- it may only need five or ten minutes of this to have a permanent effect.

> Georgia Marvin is a senior trainer and legacy holder with the Hakomi Education Network. Her focus is on mentoring teachers and trainers in the Refined Method, supporting international trainings and maintaining the link between students of Hakomi and the founder, Ron Kurtz.

The Process As Three Phases

by Georgia Marvin

To heal is to be whole again.

Preface

Ron Kurtz wrote a section in his 2010 Training Handbook for the Refined Hakomi Method called "The Process as Three Phases and Six Skill Sets in Detail." Although his article was in point form, it contains an outline of the process of practising Hakomi that is very important for both students and practitioners to understand. As a trainer, I use Ron's description of the Three Phases to structure some of my teaching and to help my students understand how to locate themselves in the process.

This paper is intended to make Ron's article more known and to expand on the point form format. Any errors are my own. I will use Ron's headings as a guide to the reader and will quote him frequently.

> *"The impulse to heal is real and powerful and lies within the client. Our job is to evoke that healing power, to meet its tests and needs and to support it in its expression and development. We are not the healers. We are the context in which healing is inspired."*

An Introduction to The Three Phases

Ron describes three distinct phases in a full Hakomi session: Preparation, Assisted Self Study and Mental-Emotional Healing Process. He writes

> *"All three phases operate within a context characterized by an embodiment within a set of well defined principles."*

For a complete discussion of those principles, please refer to the chapter on Loving Presence and the Hakomi Principles of this manual.

As a practitioner of Hakomi, it is helpful to be able to locate yourself in the three phases because each phase has its own characteristics and techniques and you can become more confident in your work if you understand the purpose and techniques of each phase.

The first phase, Preparation, involves many facets including managing your own state of mind as a practitioner, tracking and contact skills, developing safety and relationship; however, it does not involve experiments. As a learner of the method, you can rest in the first phase without needing to experiment or without jumping into experimentation too quickly. You can learn to trust this phase and get a feel for when the client is ready for transition into the second phase. The first phase is very important but not experimental.

The second phase, Assisted Self Study, is fully experimental and one of its characteristics that a practitioner needs to be comfortable with is being in the unknown, not knowing what is coming next. It requires an experimental mindset without forcing the client, an adherence to non-violence and skillful means to follow the adaptive unconscious.

The third phase, Mental-emotional Healing Process, begins when you are clear that you are working with a belief structure and your work becomes more focused. This phase of the work contains experiments but the therapist is working with a particular structure that has arisen and is challenging that structure by offering potential nourishment and the missing experience.

A Detailed Description of each Phase
Phase One. Preparation

Ron separates the first phase into two parts, loving presence and developing a healing relationship. Loving presence is *"highly dependent on your own state of mind skills"* and it is a practice. In studying Hakomi, loving presence exercises are the first practices that a student might encounter and in many trainings, it is one of the basic exercises that is used in a group at the beginning of the day or the beginning of a workshop. This essential Hakomi practice emerges from the wisdom traditions which inform our work – the search for inspiration, the expression of appreciation, the opening of the heart to love and compassion – these are some of the basic skills upon which Hakomi rests. As we sit in loving presence, we are also tracking for signs of a person's present moment experience. When I am teaching students, I ask them if they have ever been in the present of a dead person. Many have. I ask them to remember how much is absent when a person dies, how still and quiet they are, how the essence that imbued them with life is gone, dramatically gone. In contrast to the state of death, we are in the face of living beings who are in motion all the time, they are alive and uniquely so. I ask students to notice signs of life…there are many, too many to name but we learn to choose some of those signs of life and name them with short contact statements. These tracking and contacting skills are essential and in the forefront in the first phase of Hakomi and they are used throughout the process. In addition to noticing signs of present moment experience, Ron instructs us to *"make initial observations of the person's qualities,"* more enduring aspects of a person's being that he named as indicators in his later writings. The tracking of indicators is done internally without the client's awareness – it is useful information to gather before setting off into the unknown of the second phase.

The second part of the Preparation Phase is development of a healing relationship which requires a number of specific skills. A Hakomi practitioner must have good relational skills.

> *"These are skills that build and maintain a strong connection with people. Through your behavior and a few short, accurate, non-disruptive contact statements, you show that you are aware of what the other person is presently experiencing. Getting and staying in contact is the primary skill for connecting and staying connected. It creates the sense in others that you are with them, aware of their feelings and present experiences. It makes you able to anticipate their needs and work to provide help."*

Ron is specific about these connecting skills in his article called "The Six Skill Sets" which is the subsequent essay in this series.

As well as relational skills, a Hakomi practitioner needs to understand clearly that the one important relationship in a session is between your adaptive unconscious and that of the client. It is a dance, a deep dance between your non cognitive realms and the deeper realms of your client. You must learn to trust the process, to trust in the capacity for healing in your client, for the natural unfolding of that healing process and allow yourself into the flow of it all (Kurtz, Readings, 2010, p.19). Ron writes

Process & Structure

> *"This phase requires relating to the adaptive unconscious, looking for signs of cooperation and non-cooperation, making adjustments to the person's unconscious needs."*

It is not in the client's best interests to proceed into the experimental phase of the process if the adaptive unconscious is not in agreement. Once you detect signs of cooperation with the adaptive unconscious, Ron suggests that you proceed. Knowing what to do next is of course dependent on the silent tracking which you were doing in phase one and in particular tracking for indicators.

Phase Two. Assisted Self-Study.

Ron outlines six ideas in phase two: a search for indicators, development of hypotheses, development of experiments, working with outcomes of experiments (get the data, he used to say), arising of insight in the client and finally the spontaneous movement into the third phase of mental and emotional healing.

Let's examine each of these facets of the second phase. The search of indicators begins in the first phase and continues in the second phase. You do need to make observations and have ideas for experiments before starting the second phase because one hallmark of phase two is its experimental nature. In the second phase, the client is now actively self-studying and the therapist needs to have a good idea of what to study. In Ron's final years, he taught his students to search for indicators as a key skill in practicing Hakomi. He did not want to be prescriptive about the meanings of indicators: he encouraged students to be creative, to see what was there and to imagine what it might mean. He has written about indicators and offered a list of indicators, but he did not encourage his students to use lists. He wanted people to just look and see what was there, what was enduring and evident in posture, facial expressions, tone of voice, pacing, gestures, qualities and style.

When I am teaching, I use a literary metaphor to help explain indicators. One of the enduring metaphors in storytelling is the hidden door, the door in the garden wall that cannot be seen, the door that will

Process & Structure

only be seen or be opened with patience and knowledge and even perhaps some magic. Indicators are like hidden doors – you need to practice and be patient in order to see them; you need deep patience and safety for the door to open. When the door opens, it is like magic, the healing unfolds in a natural way.

Once you observe an indicator, Ron suggests that you *"develop an hypothesis about the person's models of self and world."* He elaborates this idea in "The Six Skill Sets" as "modelling skills." He says:

"The bridge between observation and experiment is the ability to create models of the laws governing the behavior you're observing. We could call these skills modelling skills. This is the method of science. Richard Feynman, the Nobel physicist, tells us the three steps of science are: make a guess, calculate the implications of your guess, and test your guess on the basis of your calculations. ...We use our ability of observe behavior, especially indicators and our knowledge of indicators, to make guesses about the person's beliefs and models of self and the world. Then we test our guesses by doing experiments.... The general idea of modelling is this: we need to make guesses about what beliefs (models) are organizing the client's behavior and we need to do that by observing that behavior."

The next step is to

"Develop and do an experiment with the indicator you've chosen to work with. These experiments are done with the person in a state of mindfulness in order to bring the actions of the adaptive unconscious into awareness. The goals of such experiments are two-fold: bringing the person's unconscious models into consciousness and initiating phase three, Mental-Emotional Healing. Experiments can be attempts to offer a kind of mental-emotional nourishment that your hypothesis predicts the person will either have difficulty accepting or will

> *experience as very nourishing. The experiment can be a way of working with an indicator for which we have no hypothesis."*

Once you have done an experiment with an indicator, you need to get the data, the result of the experiment. You can get information about the outcome of your experiment either by observing it or by getting a verbal report from the person. Given the outcome of the experiment, you have a choice of what to do next. You can refine or reject your original hypothesis about the person's models of the world. You can do another experiment based on the outcome of the previous one. The cyclical nature of the second phase, experiment, data, new experiment, refining of hypotheses, continues until there is some clarity about the client's belief systems.

Clarity comes because *"the person's models of self and the world become conscious and clear to him/her or the process moves spontaneously into the healing phase."*

This is a point in the phrasing of Hakomi that some students will miss because they are not clear about identifying models of the world or belief structures. Once this point of clarity or focus is reached, we move into the third phase.

Phase Three. The Healing Phase

This phase requires support for healing skills. The therapist must be skilled in supporting spontaneous management behaviors, in allowing time for the client's internal processing which is often in silence, in following those spontaneous behaviors, in providing comfort and holding when needed and with permission, and creating and offering missing experiences.

This phase is marked by emotional expression, strong beliefs, early memories and insight. The behavior that is displayed is controlled by the adaptive unconscious and sometimes the unconscious hijacks the client. The behavior of the adaptive unconscious is non conscious, fast, unintentional, uncontrollable and effortless. These behaviors are and were adaptive and usually learned early or under extreme conditions.

"During the third phase, the primary tasks for the practitioner are supporting the person's spontaneous management behaviors. Examples of spontaneous behaviors are changes in posture such as closing up or dropping the head, spontaneous protective thoughts, tightening certain muscles such as the shoulders, chest and stomach, and holding the breath. When these behaviors arise, we need to provide signals of safety and caring such as gentle touch, being calm, softening the voice and having a natural sympathetic facial expression, providing tissues, providing physical support when needed and accepted.

The therapist during this tender phase must contain the unfolding process by taking charge and directing the person's behavior where necessary. We need to learn to follow up on the person's spontaneous images, memories, impulses and ideas as if these were signals from the person's adaptive unconscious as to where the process wants to go.

We need to recognize periods when the person needs you to be silent by watching for signs in the face that the person is doing internal work, waiting while the person has his/her eyes closed, waiting until he/she looks directly at you and speaks before you speak, listening to the person's report about his/her insights, feelings and memories and avoiding interrupting the process by not encouraging conversation. As therapists, we provide physical and verbal comforting and nourishment. We provide the missing experience, the experience that was blocked by the person's adaptations and distorted or unrealistic models of self and the world. We allow the session to come to completion in a natural way when it feels right and when the person signals that he/she feels complete."

The Process as Six Skill Sets

"I asked him, Do you know what gyroscopic precession is?
He replied, No!
So I said, But you can ride a bicycle, right?
He said, Yes, of course!
Well, I told him, That's my point."

Riding a bicycle is a skill. One theory that explains certain behaviors of a bicycle in motion is the theory of gyroscopic precession. It tells you about the behavior of gyroscopes and why the wheels of moving bicycles are similar. It explains why a moving bicycle turns when you lean. But, you don't need to know the theory at all in order to ride well. You only have to know how bikes act, which is very easy to learn from experience. With experience, you build a model that predicts how the world acts. Habits are expressions of these models and they are functions of procedural memory and the adaptive unconscious. To ride you need skills, not theory.

I've summarized the skills needed for the Hakomi Method and organized them into six basic skill sets. If you learn and practice these, you have a very good chance of becoming competent in the method. Although each skill is unique and can be learned and practised separately, they function within a session as an integrated whole. Here are the six sets in outline:

1. State of Mind Skills

The main skill in this first set is a combination of two very important habits that create one's state of mind. The preferred state of mind is called *loving presence* and it is an integrated combination of attitude, emotional state and focus of attention. These skills help a practitioner develop a state of mind and being that is expressed effortlessly through one's demeanor and actions. This state of mind has a profound effect on the development of relationships. Of all six sets, this is the most important. Reaching and maintaining a present-centered, loving state is the first task of the therapist. Learning to do this is an essential part of the trainings. Some people are already good at this and are naturally drawn to the work.

Learning how to look and listen to someone with the intention to find something that inspires and maintains compassion, as well as the habit of staying completely focused on what's happening in the present, are the basic skills.

Being present means keeping your mind focused on what is going on for you and the client *right now*, moment to moment. To train your mind to be present like that, you have to train it away from one of our strongest, most common habits, the habit of gathering information through asking questions and conducting ordinary conversations. Those are bad habits if you're trying to be present. So, you have to train your mind not to get drawn away from present experience by getting overly focused on ideas, stories and conversation. Other skills in this set are *being patient, being and staying calm*.

Without these habits of state of being, not much in the way of a connection to a client and his or her adaptive unconscious will be possible. Without that connection, the process goes very slowly, if it moves at all.

2. Relational Skills

These are skills that build and maintain a strong connection with people. The principle ones are all about demonstrating these relational qualities and attributes. Through your behavior and a few short, accurate, non-disruptive *contact statements*, you show that you are aware of what the other person is presently experiencing. Getting and staying in contact is the primary skill for connecting and staying connected. It creates the sense in others that you are with them, aware of their feelings and present experiences. It makes you able to anticipate their needs and work to provide help.

Through your tone of voice, pace, posture and gestures, you show that you are patient, sympathetic and non-judgmental. Your body movements, facial expressions, head movements and gestures show that you understand what the person is saying, thinking and feeling. You work to gain a general understanding of the person's present situation and history. You build a model in your mind that makes sense of the way they feel, think and organize their life.

You make a habit of keeping silent when the client needs time to think and remember. You develop ways to intervene to move the process forward when needed.

3. Observational Skills

What's needed most is a *good set of attentional and recognition skills*: keeping your attention focused on present behaviors, regularly scanning the face and body for signs of present experience, regularly scanning the other's behavior for possible indicators of unconscious material, recognizing emotions quickly by subtle changes in tone of voice and/or facial expression, recognizing statements implied through tone of voice and gestures, being able to guess at the meaning of postures, gestures, "feeling" the emotions in others, through limbic resonance and mirroring, recognizing the client's need for silence, and finally, recognizing the signs of integration and memory processes.

4. Modelling Skills

The bridge between observation and experiment is the ability to create models of the laws governing the behavior you're observing. I call these skills modelling skills.

This is a method of science. Richard Feynman, the Nobel physicist, tells us the three steps of science are:

"make a guess, calculate the implications of your guess, and test your guess on the basis of your calculations."

"If my guess is true, then if I do this, this will happen." That's the gist of it. We use our ability to observe behavior, especially indicators and our knowledge of indicators, to make guesses about the person's beliefs and models of self and their world. Then we test our guesses by doing experiments. The outcomes of our experiments allow us to evaluate and refine our guesses.

There is a mathematical theorem that describes how perceptions and sensory models of the world are continuously updated in the nervous system. It's called Bayes Theorem, after the mathematician who discovered it (Frith, 2007). It describes mathematically how models and beliefs are changed in the face of new evidence. It helps us understand how some models can be believed so strongly and it suggests to me how models (beliefs) can become so strong in the face of contradictory evidence or no evidence at all.

The way we use the scientific method in Hakomi and the idea that all behavior is organized is to be able to sense some general qualities of the client, to get a feel for who the person is and how he or she learned to be in the world. And we need to constantly refine our models by continuing to make new observations and to do new experiments.

5. Experimental Skills

You need certain skills to create and execute good experiments. You must create hypotheses about core material from your observations of the client, you help the client become mindful when doing experiments, you create and execute experiments. You describe how you'd like the client to participate, you get permission, ask for mindfulness and wait for signs or a signal that mindfulness is occurring. You do the experiment, observe its outcome or ask what happened if the results are not forthcoming. You learn to follow the spontaneous reactions to an experiment and use them to support the unfolding healing process. With the results of an experiment, you design another experiment and you use the outcomes of experiments to think about missing experiences.

6. Support for Healing Skills.

You must learn to support spontaneous management behaviors. You learn to give the client time for her internal processing. You must be comfortable with silence. You must follow the spontaneous behaviors that arise in the person. You and your assistants provide comfort and holding when needed and with permission. You understand how to create and offer missing experiences and you understand that all missing experiences are missing in the present moment, they are missing because of the ways in which a client is organized to meet the world.

The Process in Graphic Form

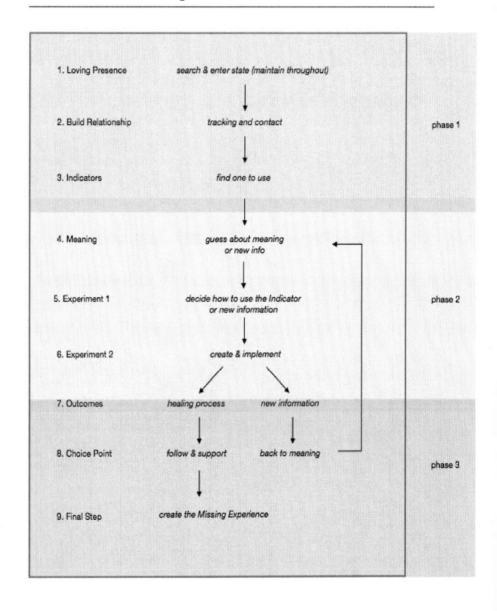

Logic of the Method

1. Observe the person's nonverbal behaviors and make a guess
    a. Observe: indicators (habitual, adaptive qualities)
    b. Guess about the person's models of self and world
    c. Look for models which may be causing unnecessary suffering

2. Calculate (reason) the implications of your guess
    a. Based on your observations, what experiment might you do?
    b. Based on your guess about the person's model of self and the world, what is your prediction about the person's reaction to your experiment?

3. Test your prediction by setting up and doing an experiment
    a. Offer a potentially nourishing experiment based on your predictions

4. Observe or get a report about the outcome of the experiment.
    a. Get the data

5. Refine your ideas about the person's models
    a. Recalculate your predictions, based on the errors in your previous predictions.

6. Test the new prediction with a new experiment

7. Recognizing evidence of a correct prediction
    a. Main evidence: a reaction to an experiment which is either emotional, surprising, and/or rejects the offered nourishment in some way

Process & Structure

8. If a healing process begins
    a. Support the process
    b. Follow the clues offered by the adaptive unconscious
    c. Those clues are spontaneous, possibly surprising, and of interest to the person in the healing process

9. Support the person's spontaneous emotional management behaviors

Skillful Hakomi

The essays in this collection are from the 2010 Readings in the Hakomi Method and from the 2010 Training Handbook. Advanced students of Hakomi will appreciate the subtle descriptions of Hakomi therapy as well as Ron's reflections on the common habits that cause failure.

> From the Readings 2010

The Dance

I've been reading Moshe Feldenkrais's book *"The Illusive Obvious"* again. I read it years ago and it was so illusive that I didn't get it at all. This time, I got some of it. So let me tell you what Moshe says in the introduction. It's important for us.

He talks about how he first learned to work with people. He was studying with a man named Jacoby and Jacoby gave him this analogy as a description of his work: Jacoby said, "Suppose, there is a woman who really knows how to dance. She's at a dance hall and she notices a man who's not dancing. She goes over and asks him to dance and he says, 'No! I really don't know how to dance.' She says, 'Come on! Come on!' And she gets him to try. They just start dancing. No instructions. She doesn't tell him what to do. She doesn't tell him which steps to make or anything like that. He learns just by moving with her and feeling her movements. Eventually, he starts feeling the rhythms and the movements. He starts moving with her. And, after a little while—say, fifteen, twenty minutes—he's dancing." That's what Jacoby told Moshe.

Moshe says that's how he does therapy. He starts to "dance" with the person's nervous system. He moves the person's body until the person's nervous system gets the dance that Moshe is doing with it. It's not instruction in the verbal sense. Moshe doesn't talk to the person. It may be a physical version of limbic resonance. Maybe it's cerebellum resonance. I would call it an exchange of sensitivities. Interacting this way, the person learns a new and better way to use his body. He learns by feeling and being felt by someone who knows a better way.

We can make an analogy with our own work and with psychotherapy in general. Seen this way, it becomes more interesting and more enjoyable. The therapist is just being who he or she is, whatever that is. The client is learning to be with the therapist. They are learning to be with each other, but the therapist has special training and skills for being with people. So, the two of them learn to relate in a way that changes them both. Dancing with an expert teaches you to dance. Being in therapy with an expert develops your capacity to be mindful, to be calm, to understand yourself, to release yourself from painful memories and thoughtless actions, to relate in ways that are realistic and satisfying. The therapy seen this way is a dance of teacher and student.

It's not a dance of movements; it's a dance of states of mind. If you're in a compassionate state of mind, if you're in loving presence, it helps the client open up and feel himself. It helps clients to release emotions and memories into consciousness. This approach is different from the release of muscular blocks in the body. That kind of release is part of what body psychotherapies work on. That approach started with Wilhelm Reich, based on his idea of "muscular armor." Body psychotherapists look for "blocks to expression," especially blocks to emotional expression. So when you go to a bioenergetic therapist, you're going to beat on the bed in order to express and feel your anger. It's an old idea in physiology: feeling follows action. The bioenergetic therapist looks at you and they say, "Okay let's do this!" They bend you back over a stool to release the blocks to expressing fear and things like that. If they see signs of unexpressed anger, they are going to do something very physical to bring about its expression. For them, the expression is physically blocked. In Gestalt, the method is to ask the client to exaggerate his actions. Both are looking for a way to bring the emotions into consciousness.

In Hakomi, we only do some of that. We work to bring painful beliefs into consciousness and the memories, ideas and emotions come right along with them. We're interested in these ideas and memories, not because they are mostly out of awareness, which they are. We're interested in them because they control what can be thought, perceived and taken in as emotional nourishment. For us, the main things are the blocks to taking in the healthy, nourishing things of the world and becoming conscious of the unconscious motives that keep one from doing so. This also comes into consciousness spontaneously when therapist and client are in the right kinds of states of mind.

I never liked the idea of banging on the bed—and I've done my share. I never got to my anger that way. I'm much too nice a guy. I got to it when John Pierrakos was pushing so hard on my face that I suddenly and spontaneously decided to kill him on the spot. That's how he got me to my anger. I didn't think for a second about the consequences. If he hadn't gone to the farthest corner of the room before I could open my eyes and get my hands around his neck, I might be banging on rocks with a sledge hammer (which I'm sure could evolve into an expression of anger). John, from the far corner of the room, merely said, "The murderer." Well, he got that right. And I'm grateful, too! It felt like coming home. I was much less afraid after that, more willing to take chances.

Now, back to my theme:

Instead of taking action to bring awareness and understanding, we work to create a state of mind that has the same outcomes. The state is mindfulness and a willingness to experiment with one's reactions. The therapist is in a loving, curious and creative state of mind. The client is in a vulnerable and self-observing state of mind. A kind of harmony must exist between these states. Creating that harmony is the first task of the therapist. It's called building a healing relationship. It could just as easily be called, "the dance."

It takes a kind of faith to work this way. The woman in Jacoby's story had faith that he could learn just by dancing with her, faith in his intelligence and sincerity. We have that kind of faith also, and in the innate goodness of people and in their ability to heal emotional wounds. Just as people heal physically, they also heal emotionally. One way they do that is by being with people who can dance with emotional pain, with beliefs that cause suffering. We know that dance.

People come to psychotherapy for all kinds of reasons. Here's what they get from the Hakomi method. Here's the dance we're doing: we help people discover how they habitually and unconsciously organize painful experiences. We help them experience new and more satisfying ways to be and do. When we do that, people learn to understand themselves and change.

To support self-discovery, we use mindfulness. For mindfulness, we need safety. For safety, we need loving presence. All of that is part of the dance. And, we need to see and feel who the client is. For that, we have to train ourselves. We need to focus on the nonverbal, the storyteller, not just the story. Verbal communication is almost always a story of some kind. Or it's analysis and explanation. It's abstract, not about present experience. Or, it's a search for causes. None of that is helpful when we're trying to discover how we organize experience. What is helpful is bringing attention to present experience and experimenting with it, dancing with it.

The client's mood and emotions change from one moment to the next as do the client's posture, facial expressions, tone of voice and gestures. As a therapist who is looking for something to experiment with, this is your field of interest. From what you see and hear in the present moment, you can easily find something to experiment with. You can work with anything that seems juicy or unusual. Every moment, experience is being organized. Focusing on an experience in itself brings us in touch with the beliefs and memories that are organizing it.

To help the clients experience more satisfying ways of organizing their experience, we discover the kinds of emotional nourishment that are generally available but aren't being taken in. It's like finding the dance steps that the client hasn't learned yet or is afraid to take. When we discover something like this, we experiment with it by offering that exact nourishment. We take the steps until the client learns to step with us. That is what the client eventually discovers, that he can do and feel those things that once seemed impossible and that they feel good. The missing experience is a dance step one was afraid to take, hadn't even imagined. Once the emotional nourishment is accepted, we practice a little.

Which missing experiences do we support? We support a balance between spontaneous, nonviolent, satisfying expression of all emotions. However, we emphasize what in Buddhism is called the higher emotions: loving kindness, sympathetic joy and equanimity. That's the sweetest dance there is.

From the Readings 2010

On Being A Portal

"Portal: (noun) An entrance or a means of entrance." (American Heritage Dictionary of the English Language, 2016)

"He who wants to do good, knocks at the gate; he who loves finds the gates open." (Sri Rabindranath Tagore Thakur, 1861-1941)

"Where love rules, there is no will to power and where power predominates, there love is lacking. The one is the shadow of the other." (Jung, 1943)

"The detection of a person as safe or dangerous triggers neurobiologically determined prosocial or defensive behaviors." (Porges, 2004)

Porges uses music, played through headphones and limited in frequency range to the range of the human voice, to trigger what he has named as The Social Engagement System (SES). In normal, everyday situations, the SES functions to enhance human-to-human communication. This complex neurobiological system activates when the situation calls for such communication and when the situation is perceived as being safe. The reason the SES can be triggered by range limited music is that listening to such music causes the middle ear to narrow a person's range of hearing to those same frequencies. This action of the middle ear is just one of the functions of the SES. Other functions include smiling and looking directly at someone - regulation of the larger nervous system in support of all prosocial behaviors. Porges talks about the middle ear function as "a portal to the system."

It is a gateway to a state of mind, based upon a specific configuration of the entire nervous system, a state of mind that is prosocial and not defensive. Porges treats autistic children by triggering their social engagement systems through stimulation of the middle ear. Often, in only a few sessions of forty-five minutes each, the SES is activated, and the child's behavior changes from distant and defensive to more relaxed and social.

I watched as Porges worked with a woman who was being stimulated by range limited music equipment. I saw the changes that could happen in a half hour. When the woman was done, I put the headphones on and listened to the same taped music she had. I felt the changes it produced in me: I felt very loving towards everyone in the room. After about ten minutes, I took the headphones off and did some Hakomi work with that same woman Porges had worked with. After ten or fifteen minutes, which included some intense moments between us, her feelings changed from a baseline of sadness, isolation, loneliness, anger and hopelessness to a feeling of connection with me — a warm, appreciative and nourishing state: social engagement. In this state, she was able to experience what for her were new, positive feelings and hopes. Porges, who'd been watching me work, said to me afterwards, something like, "You're a portal." I must have looked puzzled, because he elaborated, "Just like the music."

He meant that my behavior had brought the woman's SES on line. My behaviors, tone of voice, facial expressions, pace, attitude, my entire presence with her, the fact that my attention never wavered, the constant kindness that I felt and demonstrated — all these were such that she changed her state of mind. I like to call this kind of engagement loving presence. Something about me, a deliberate, constant feeling of compassion for the person before me gave me the potential to evoke her social engagement. I became a gateway for her to go from one state of mind to another. I was a portal.

It's nothing new that we trigger one another, that emotions are communicable. Fear or rage can spread through a crowd or escalate in an exchange between two people. There's nothing new about this. Nor is it new that we can be portals for each other's loving, prosocial states. What is new and important to recognize is that loving presence can be a powerful force for change, in everyday life or as a part of psychotherapy. A therapist whose state of mind is loving presence offers his clients a portal, through which their perceptions, moods and self-knowledge can change in positive ways. The most important thing is not "the power to change" people, it's not technique or method, not confrontation, reason, cognition or conditioning. The most important thing is just what it has always been, an opening of oneself to include the being and well being of another. The important thing, the effective thing, is to open yourself, to become a gateway through which the love that is present in you can welcome the love that has been waiting in another.

> *'Smile at each other; smile at your wife, smile at your husband, smile at your children, smile at each other — it doesn't matter who it is — and that will help you to grow up in greater love for each other.'* *(Mother Teresa, 1996)*

> From the Readings 2010

Silence & Following

"The best leader follows."(Lao Tzu)

A good therapist shares control with everything present, sometimes moving deeply into to the unfolding action, sometimes waiting quietly as the other does inner work, surfing gracefully the changing amplitudes of intimacy.

I think of the Hakomi Method differently now - my vision of the work has changed from the idea of "doing psychotherapy" to assisting in another's self-study. The work is still mindfulness-based, it's still experiential and experimental and nonviolent. All those things were there at the beginning. But something very important has been added. It has shifted for me. It's no longer about curing disease. It's now about freedom and a change in one's experience of self. This refined method tries to help people discover things about themselves, the most important things. The method brings new understanding to the conscious mind. As we do experiments in mindfulness, memories and emotions arise which are often surprising to the client. They can be very different from what the client may have expected. During those moments the client is dealing with something that takes time to absorb. During those moments, the client needs time to feel and think.

Those moments after an experiment are times when silence is the most helpful thing a therapist can do. There are other times when silence is used, but these are the most important. We have to give them that time. Thankfully, it is very easy to recognize when clients need that. Typically, they close their eyes and tip their heads forward a little. Their faces show signs that they are thinking and having insights. They are busy integrating the new information. After something surprising and important, that's totally natural. We have to be silent then and give the person time. As always, being tuned in and responding to what the person needs in the moment, we gain the cooperation of the unconscious.

Silence is also appropriate after a contact statement. This is about following. We want to help the client discover unconscious beliefs and memories. For that, we need to let the adaptive unconscious lead. It leads us by bringing memories, emotions, impulses, images, tensions and ideas into consciousness. For the client, they arise spontaneously as part of the flow of experience in reaction to whatever is going on externally and internally as a chain of associations. Metaphorically, we can say that the adaptive unconscious is giving this to us. We can treat these as pointing to where the process wants to go. A healing process tends to go towards memories and insights, and usually deep feelings. The spontaneous moments make clear what we might do next; in that way, they lead and we follow.

Often, therapists feel that they have to lead. They feel responsible for "making things happen". So, they're active, busy talking and questioning, and running things. That sense of one's role and the activity it fosters all too often interrupts the slow, natural flow of the healing process. Silence and following are very different.

Here's an example from a session I did: after I gave the client a probe she reported an impulse to collapse. She leaned a little to her left and dropped her head. She said, "I feel like falling to the floor." She seemed a little surprised at her impulse and curious about it. I suggested that she go ahead and do it, fall towards the floor. And I added, and notice what happens next. This is my idea of following. She does it and as she does it, I remain silent. As she lies there with her eyes closed, not moving, I am silent. I wait for the unconscious to give us the next thing. After a minute or so, she becomes very sad. I contact it. "Sadness now, huh." Then I wait in silence as she learns for herself about her sadness. If she wants support, I'll have someone sit next to her, maybe put a hand on her shoulder or back. I remain silent, waiting for the next thing to happen. If the emotion deepens, I may have someone physically support whatever the client is doing to manage her emotions, like holding herself together or covering her face. After that's been arranged, I again wait quietly while this new situation develops. In a few moments, a painful memory emerges, a memory that needed time to emerge and more to develop. A client needs time to feel into it, to grasp how it shaped her life, and more time to resolve the confusions and pain the original events created. Time and silence.

All along, the adaptive unconscious has been leading and I have been following. Following creates the need for silence and waiting for what the unconscious will give us next. At these moments, I am not trying to make things happen. I am letting them happen. At other times, I am active. I'm making contact statements and doing experiments. But, once material begins emerging spontaneously, once the healing process begins to flow, I switch to silence and following. The unconscious leads and I follow.

Moving the Process Forward

Move the process forward when the interaction becomes conversational or when the client is continuously talking about anything but his or her present experience.

How to move it forward?
- contact something in the present moment, the client's experience or behavior
- talk about noticing an indicator and suggest an experiment
- interrupt storytelling, explaining, questioning, abstract discussions, conversations

When to use silence effectively:
- when the client is processing internally. Some of the signs of internal self-awareness are eyes closed, facial and head movements, deep concentration, emotions arising
- when the client is describing present moment experience

Habits as Causes of Failure

> *"We tend to seek easy, single-factor explanations of success. For most important things, though, success actually requires avoiding many separate possible causes of failure." (Diamond, 1997)*

This principle can certainly be applied to doing psychotherapy. A general version of the principle would be this: *"Any complex system has many ways it can fail."* The method is certainly a complex system. For it to succeed, the practitioner must have an array of useful habits and must avoid some important ones that tend to disrupt the process. There are three habits, based on very common attitudes, that inevitably cause the method to fail.

What might be a good habit in one situation can easily be a bad one in a very different situation. For the refined method, there are three all too common habits that have seriously damaging effects on the process. These are:

1. having to be in control;
2. focusing on figuring everything out; and
3. getting stuck in conversations.

Although these three are related, I'll discuss them one at a time. I'll discuss their sources in western culture and the effects they have on the process.

Habit One: Having to Be in Control

Newton's laws state that an object at rest remains at rest unless acted upon by an external force. He also stated that an object in motion continues in motion unless acted upon by an external force. In other words, things don't move on their own. An external force is always necessary. That's a good definition of a "thing". It's a serious mistake to think that living things operate the same way. Newton's laws work really well for objects possessing only mass but humans and other living things are not simply mass; they're also, to varying degrees, self-determined, aware and intelligent. They move on their own. Newton had a powerful influence on the images of reality and the philosophy of the western world. In that image, reality is made up of atoms —solid, separate, isolated, indivisible objects - billiard balls that only move when acted upon by an external force. And who or what is that force? Well, when practitioners assume it's themselves, the process goes astray. Newton also postulated that, for every action, there's an equal and opposite reaction. Use force, even if it's subtle, you're likely to get resistance. That's what makes the attitude of having to be in control a sure deal breaker. It might be a good idea to keep an eye out for defining other people's behaviors as resistance, rather than, as I prefer to see it, management.

Contrast this with the Zen Buddhist saying, *"Spring comes and the grass grows by itself"* or the quote from the *Tao Te Ching* about mastery of the world. There is a natural way that needs no interference from another person. The influence of Newtonian model on the practice of medicine was for the most part a good thing. It's just not a good model for psychotherapy, especially the assisted self study version of Hakomi. The application of a medical model leads to situations where "patients" tells their stories, describe their symptoms, are questioned, get diagnosed and are then "treated". In this model, the patient's participation is small and amounts to little more than following orders, except of course for the very organic healing that occurs.

In most forms of psychotherapy, this is the underlying philosophy. The client needs to be moved and the moving force is the therapist. Consider the concepts of resistance and defenses. What's left out of this philosophy is the whole notion of people as self-organizing and self-healing. What stands in contrast to the external force concept is the internal force of the client's own healing impulses and powers. In the newer organic models and in Hakomi, the therapist provides support for those inner processes. The practitioner in the refined model is someone who provides support for the organic healing processes of the client, rather than being a force controlling the actions of an object. A good book to read is *The Heart and Soul of Change: What Works in Therapy* (Duncan, Miller, Wampold and Hubble, 2010)

Negative Effects of Habit One

When the therapist has the belief, conscious or implicit, that he or she has to control the process, this can easily result in overt or covert resistance or contrarily, in submission and passivity on the part of the client. Whichever happens, from that point on the client's natural healing processes are not guiding the process. The result is a drawn out process that wastes time and energy.

Alternatives

A therapist's belief in the client's power to heal through an inner directed healing process, and the therapist's knowledge of how to set the stage for that process to unfold will lead to much better results. There is a dance that takes place between the whole practitioner and the whole client, based to a large degree on the beliefs and emotional underpinnings of each person's motivations. It's a dance of mutuality. Control flows both ways. Acceptance is present in each dancer. This kind of therapy is not run by the emotional operating system for dominance. It's run by the ones for social bonding and care. That's when it works best. This approach is not for everyone. It's only for people with enough emotional maturity and self awareness to operate within such a framework.

The key to working without having to be in control is recognizing what will initiate and support a person's healing, supplying just that, and then letting things take their natural course. That means anticipating that a natural healing process will emerge and knowing how to help it emerge. It means observing, following and supporting that kind of process and operating from this larger intention. To let things take their natural course, one must come from loving presence, loving, attentive, patient, observant and present for the other. And, when you're really attuned, it means being at one with the situation. It means being with another while holding the clear, durable intention to dance a healing dance.

Habit Two: Focusing on Figuring Everything Out

<u>Meditatio</u>
When I carefully consider the curious habits of dogs,
I am compelled to conclude
That man is the superior animal.
When I consider the curious habits of man,
I confess, my friend, I am puzzled.
(Ezra Pound)

Well, I'm more than a little puzzled myself about the idea that humans are, or even could be, rational animals. Damasio (2003) wrote a whole book about how useless reason is without emotions to give values to its application.

There are many good reasons for peace in the world, but reason won't suffice to bring it. It will take feeling and motivated effort, and enough love for ourselves and for each other to be kind and caring towards all humanity. That's a tall order, I admit, but it's also not something we can afford to fail at. So it's worth a serious look at the possible causes of failure.

Negative Effects of Habit Two

When we start with the implicit belief that the client's behavior is a puzzle to unravel, when we act like we have to figure these things out, before we do anything, we generally ask questions and follow up questions and, in our minds, we search for the sources of the client's suffering in the answers, explanations and stories of the client. When our approach is mostly thinking like this, the whole process gets skewed into the abstract. The assumption is that thinking is our primary tool. This approach is sometimes called, "leading with your head".

Alternatives

For the kind of intimate and subtle connection that encourages another's healing, more than thinking is required. Our job is to provide two things:

- a context that stimulates and supports the client's natural healing processes and
- a way to help initiate that process.

For the first, loving presence, careful observation and a lot of experience with nonverbal indicators are what's needed. The focus of attention needs to be constant, careful observation. The habit of figuring things out takes too much consciousness away from that. For the second thing, stimulating a healing process, setting up and doing little experiments in mindfulness is just the thing. Doing good experiments is a very effective way to bring feelings, beliefs and memories out of the unconscious, so that healing old hurts can begin.

When the client realizes how and why he habitually organizes his experience the way he does, change becomes possible.

Habit Three: Getting Stuck in Conversations

This habit is related to the other two. They're both part of a larger pattern which Francisco Varela called "the abstract attitude." I believe he meant the general bias towards thinking rather than sensing and feeling and not focusing on present experience.

We have moved out of our long history of living in small groups, knowing everyone and communicating face-to-face. We now communicate, to a large extent by phone and even more perhaps, by email, and very often with people we've never met or don't know very well. Communication in these cases is generally limited to words. This limitation helps create our habit of nearly complete reliance on language as a means for gathering information about people. We're not the only social species. Others, like wolves, ants, bees and musk oxen, communicate successfully without words. It is our habit of relying on questions and answers and talking about what is not present that is, in the context of assisting in anther's self discovery, a bad habit.

Negative Effects of Habit Three

The main negative effect engaging in a lot of conversation with our clients — especially conversations where the therapist asks a lot of questions and the client mostly just answer them — has the effect of preventing rather than promoting the client's natural healing process. It may even keep it from happening at all. Consider this example: the client starts to feel sad and says so. The therapist replies, "What are you sad about?" Or even, "Why do you feel that way?" If the client starts to think about reasons or explanations for his sadness, he loses contact with it. This kind of thing happens all the time. I see this in ordinary conversations people have. I see it in the kind of psychotherapy portrayed in movies and on television. I sometimes see it when I supervise Hakomi students and practitioners who haven't trained with me personally. The sadness the client feels is the beginning of a healing process. The proper response to it can lead to an emotion deepening into memories, release and the possibility of resolution and integration. Ordinary conversation interrupts an emotional healing process.

When the therapist asks one question after another, the client become passive, answering each question and then waiting for the next one. This approach rarely leads to healing. Mostly it ends up as a conversation and not much else. Explanations and conversation rarely initiate a healing process and are not particularly designed to do so.

Alternatives

All of these habits are the outcomes of a culture that promotes ego, power and control. The alternative is the use of skillful means - the therapist's state of mind and attentional skills, and all the techniques that make up the method.

Refinements

Original Components, (Kurtz 1997)

Character Theory: This derived from my interest in Bioenergetics and the work of Wilhelm Reich. It was taught both as theory and method in the original trainings held in Vermont, Connecticut and Colorado in the late 70's and early 80's.

Reading Bodies (Posture and Structure): This was a direct outcome of studying Bioenergetics and Reich. I would ask people to stand and I'd look at them for the kinds of bodily signs talked about by Alexander Lowen, in his many books. In 1976, Hector Prestera, M.D. and I published *The Body Reveals* about interpreting body structures.

Experiments: I learned to use these when I studied Gestalt in the late 60's at Esalen and as a teacher at San Francisco State. It was a very experimental time, with the whole culture experimenting with new ways to be and to relate.

Use of Mindfulness: Asking people to become mindful before doing an experiment was something that came out of my private practice around 1974. I was motivated by the idea that people in mindfulness could observe their reactions and begin to understand their true beliefs about themselves and the world, the beliefs that organize their behavior and experience. This was and is a direct way to support self-study and self-discovery. My meditation practice, a retreat with Chögyam Trungpa, and workshops with Moshe Feldenkrais and Ruthy Alon were all part the inspiration.

Nonviolence: This inspiration also came in the 60's. Partly it was the temper of the times, the Vietnam war, Flower Children and a couple of years of teaching at San Francisco State. It was the coming of Buddhism to America, my love of the Tao Te Ching and the anti-war movement. To me, nonviolence means not persisting, not forcing anything, not using power or coercion or acting authoritarian. This sentiment was the main reason I gave up using bioenergetic methods.

Tracking and Contact: Of course contact came from Rogerian Therapy which I read about in graduate school and taught later in college. The idea of tracking, of constantly following the trajectory of people's present experience, was a reflection of my Navy experience as a fire control radar operator. "Tracking" is what those radars do; they follow the movements of an airplane, staying locked on it as it flies. The practice of tracking came out of that.

Probes: This technique came at the same time as the use of mindfulness. Having heard clients speak about themselves and having studied their posture and body structure, I realized that people were not always aware of what beliefs were at the core of their behavior and experience. As a way to help them discover that, I wanted to surprise them with their own reactions to statements that I figured they would not be able to accept, in spite of the fact that all those statements were designed to be potentially nourishing. Sure enough, it worked. And it became a cornerstone of the Hakomi Method.

Taking Over: This was the outcome of having pursued nonviolent ways to support the emotional processes that sometimes followed probes and other experiments. It was a simple reversal of the Bioenergetic practice of "breaking down" the defenses. I first used it in the late 70's. It quickly developed into the second major technique of the method, expanding into all kinds of ways to take over verbally and physically. It's used both in experiments done with the person in mindfulness to help people study themselves and with evoked emotional reactions, where it's used to support people's spontaneous management behaviors.

Offering Emotional Nourishment: This was a natural outcome of using potentially nourishing statements as probes. After some processing, the same offering that was automatically rejected when offered as a probe could be used to provide relief, relaxation and emotional satisfaction. It eventually became the general goal of providing missing experiences, experiences that were automatically avoided due to the beliefs that organized experience.

Touching and Comforting: This is something we do that developed with the use of assistants and a new understanding of the adaptive unconscious.

Important Concepts: These concepts were important in the early development of the method:

- Core Beliefs: Core beliefs were what we called the general organizers of experience.
- Gaining the Cooperation of the Unconscious: We thought of the unconscious much the same way as Freud and Jung did, though they certainly had their differences. Some of the ideas about this came from the work of Milton Erickson.
- Defenses: The idea of psychological defenses was and still is quite common in the field.

These eleven components make up a good portion of the original method. They came together over two and a half decades of learning, teaching and training people. Used together in an integrated way, they make an effective method for helping others with their personal growth and emotional healing. They are taught and practiced today in at least thirteen countries and used by hundreds of practitioners.

Since the early 90's, when I resigned as director of the Hakomi Institute, I have continued to refine the method and to teach these refinements in workshops and trainings along with several newer trainers who have trained and worked with me, rather than the Institute. Some of them, like Donna Martin, have been working and teaching with me for fifteen years or more. Some of the refinements were made as far back as the early 90's and some as recently as the last three months. I'd like to describe the major ones and the changes they made to the method.

The Major Refinements (Kurtz 2010)

Loving Presence: The progression of my thinking: at first, I thought mostly about techniques, the momentary interventions I'd learned from Gestalt and Bioenergetics. After thinking about these for a while, I began to see how they formed a unified method, the use and timing of the techniques and the theory that made sense of them. While thinking, teaching and writing about method and techniques, I began to see how they had to fit within the relationship one had with the client. I began to have ideas about what we called *The Healing Relationship*. All of this was part of the development of the original method. Then, after reading a book called *Human Change Process* by Michael J. Mahoney (1991), I began to see that the most important ingredient—after client factors such as motivation—was what he called *personhood or therapist personal factors*. I realized during one mind-opening session that my own state of mind (or state of being) was strongly affecting the outcome of the session. State of mind very quickly became the most important aspect of the healing relationship. I called that state of mind *loving presence* and began teaching it in trainings and workshops as the first and most important element of the method. The workshop was about how one creates that state of mind in oneself. Presence refers to attending to the flow of experience from moment to moment (Senge et al, 2005).

Using Assistants: I began using assistants in my workshops and trainings back in the 80's. When I did demonstrations, I would have one or two of the observers come and help me with taking over voices and physical management reactions. I have trained many advanced students as assistants. It's both a very good way to involve people and to teach them the method through that kind of participation. Since the mid-nineties, I've used assistants in my private practice. There are many things you can do when you have assistants that you can't do when you're alone with a client. For a while, early in 2000, I would have four clients come at a time, people who knew each other. I would work with one person at a time and have the other three assisting me. Then we'd rotate and work with the next person.

Searching for and Using Indicators: Having tracked clients' present experiences for many years, I began to notice and think about the person's habitual behaviors and qualities that are a regular part of their way of being, qualities like holding the head on an angle, shrugging the shoulders a lot, talking fast, constantly watching me, default facial expressions, and other enduring habits. There are an endless number of these significant qualities. I learned that these qualities often reflect early adaptations and are the external expressions of implicit beliefs. One of the first things I do when I start a session with someone is to search for these qualities, which I call indicators, and I design possible experiments. I don't teach character theory any more and consider character traits as just one limited subset of indicators.

Naming the work Assisted Self-Study: This is the most important refinement of all. I stopped thinking of the work as belonging within the medical model of treating psychological problems or diseases. I began to think of the method as a way of assisting a person in the pursuit of self-knowledge. When this pursuit is successful, relief from the suffering usually follows. Knowing the truth about oneself, making implicit beliefs conscious, recognizing the automatic behaviors of the adaptive unconscious, is the most direct path to changing oneself at a deep level. As part of this shift in perspective, I began to require of clients that they understand the work as self- study, that they be able to enter into mindful states and participate in the experiments that are vital to the process. I give new clients a one page description of what they can expect in a Hakomi session.

Adapting to the Adaptive Unconscious: The adaptive unconscious has come into currency in the last couple of decades. Books have been written about it (Wilson, 2002). In contrast to the Freudian unconscious, it's much more of a helpmate than a "cauldron of erotic and violent impulses". It is there to "conserve consciousness" and this is described as cognitive load theory. As I learned about the adaptive unconscious, I began to recognize and work with that part of the mind as it interprets situations and initiates actions and reactions acting completely outside of conscious decisions and awareness. Knowing this, I can understand and respond to a person's behavior in a more

Irritations: In 1903, Pierre Janet wrote about events that overwhelm a person, events that cannot be integrated and made sense of, events that happen when we're vulnerable, and especially when we're young. The emotions and memories of such events can end up, in his words, "encapsulated" in the unconscious. They remain there causing irritation and suffering and influencing emotions and behavior. It is these irritations that our experiments in mindfulness often bring into consciousness. And that's exactly what we want. Once conscious, with the proper emotional support, sense can finally be made of them and the irritation finally dissolved. (see Rossi, 1996)

Following (Using Spontaneous Impulses and Behaviors): In keeping with a new awareness of the functioning of the adaptive unconscious, I now see the spontaneous impulses and thoughts that come up during the work as signals from the adaptive unconscious which point the way the work might proceed. When something pops into a client's consciousness, an impulse or a memory, I will use it as part of the very next experiment.

Honoring the Need for Silence: One thing that stands out in the demonstrations that I do is the long amounts of time during which I am silent and waiting for the client. Observers frequently comment on this. When I work, I track for signs that the person is inside: thinking, feeling, remembering, integrating. The signs are simple. Usually the eyes are closed. The head may be turned to one side or nodding. The face may show signs that the person is thinking or having insights. When this is happening, I simply wait in silence. My attention remains on the person. When the person opens his or her eyes, I am present and I wait for the person to speak first. These simple behaviors help shape the kind of relationship we will have. They indicate that I will give the person all the time he or she needs to process experiences. This is especially important when emotions have spontaneously arisen or have arisen in reaction to an experiment. I have learned that clients need time to remember and figure things out, to integrate the memories and feelings that have arisen during the healing process. Integration is happening and needs to be protected from interruption. So, I remain silent. We remain silent to allow the person to deepen into the experience. We offer and extend comfort when those same emotions are moving freely through the person and painful memories are being integrated, which happens spontaneously if not interfered with. At those times we're silent.

Touching and Comforting: I started many years ago to offer physical contact in ways that are generally frowned upon in professional psychotherapy circles. Of course, they have good reasons for this. The imbalance of power, the privacy of the two-person interaction, the intimate nature of the relationship, all make it quite easy to violate boundaries. When I use touch and offer comfort, it is always in the presence of witnesses, sometimes a hundred or more. Usually, I'm not the one touching the person or holding them. I have assistants do that and always with permission. We touch people, usually gently on the arm or shoulder, at the first physical sign of sadness or grief, signs like tears forming and the voice changing. When we do touch, we're signaling that we're aware of the person's feelings and that we're sympathetic.

Implicit Beliefs: Beliefs are implicit when they are not recoverable as memories of events. They are memorized procedures and habits. They are equivalent to beliefs in that the habitual behaviors can be thought of as the enactment of implicit rules: "if this, then do that". They are outside of awareness, not because they are necessarily repressed; they are simply actions that can be performed without conscious attention, thus preserving consciousness for tasks which need time to think about and implement. Like all the habits that are by their nature procedural, they are functions of the adaptive unconscious. Some are adaptations to situations that were painful and/or unresolved. It is these later adaptations that we help bring into conscious awareness, in order to resolve and change them.

> Excerpts from "Eight Talks on the Refined Hakomi Method", June to November 2009. These talks were delivered in Ireland, Sheffield UK, Germany and the United States, transcribed by Trudy Walters, Gabriela Valdés Villarreal, Sophie Cattier, Arlene Cassidy, Bari Falese, John Hillman, Stuart Friedman and Merilyn Rinchen Hand.

Talks on Refined Hakomi

The Vision

My original vision of Hakomi was to teach anyone, professional and lay people. I chose to teach them because of their personal qualities. I rarely turned anybody away. I left the Hakomi Institute and resigned the directorship around 1990. It is now governed by a board of directors who have changed the vision I had. They now prefer to teach professionals. Their goal is to become part of the establishment, to become a recognized branch of psychotherapy. That's not a bad idea, but it wasn't my idea. I didn't have an advanced degree or a license to practice. I only recently received an honorary degree, 46 years after I started graduate school. I've always been a rebel.

Something that Salvador Minuchin said really touched me: "To create something new, or to begin something new, you need to oppose something that's already there." I definitely had that attitude. I tried a lot of things but I didn't like what I found - not in psychotherapy, not in Gestalt, not in Bioenergetics. I felt opposed to the violence, the tyranny of expertise, and this opposition still gives me the energy to keep creating.

A student of mine, sitting by my pool in Ashland, once said to me: "You don't give a (***) about what anybody thinks." That surprised me. I had to think about it. In a way, he's right, but I hadn't realized it when he said it. I do my own thinking. Always did. So, I accept anyone with the right personal qualities into my trainings, some of them professionals, and some of them not.

There was a famous industrialist, J.P. Morgan, who died in 1913. One of the world's biggest the banks still has his name. J.P. Morgan said, "All other things being equal, I choose the man who tastes his food before he salts it." All other things being equal, I choose a person who does what needs to be done, without being asked. I want to teach people who have the quality of being aware of what's going on, and what's needed and who habitually jump in to help. That's my criteria. If I see this in a person who has those other right qualities, I know I can train that person. I don't care about degrees.

I have a couple of quotes of my own that I particularly like:

> A good therapist shares control with everything present, sometimes moving deeply into the unfolding action, sometimes waiting quietly as the other does inner work, surfing gracefully the changing amplitudes of intimacy.

That's about being non-intrusive. You're not in control. You're sharing control with everything present. In other words, sometimes you just step in and do what has to be done and sometimes you sit back and wait.

Milton Erickson had a theory called the utilization principle (Erickson, 1980). He used anything present in his work with clients. He worked at mental hospitals. Here's an example of using everything present. He had a client who insisted he was Jesus Christ. Erickson went up to him in the hall and said, "I hear you have experience as a carpenter." The guy agreed and Ericson put him to work in the carpentry shop. He didn't try to talk the guy out of it - he just took it and used it. The work in the shop helped the fellow get well.

Here's another quote of mine about being non intrusive:

> The impulse to heal is real and powerful and lies within the client. Our job is to evoke that healing power, to meet it tests and needs and to support it in its expression and development. We are not the healers. But, we can be the context in which healing can happen. The best way to be that context is to be in loving presence, to be non-intrusive.

Over the years, my vision of the method has evolved. You'd expect that over forty years. It's evolved not only in its fine detail, but

Refinements

also in a larger sense. I see the method now more as a natural process, not something very complicated. I see it as a way someone with developed skills for caring and relating can assist someone who has the courage and intent to seek a happier way of being through self-knowledge.

Because I've been free to change things and because I kept learning, I changed things. I dropped what seemed unnecessary or added what worked better. The source of these changes, as you might suspect, was the great variety of experiences that come from working with all kinds of clients, in different cultures and the natural tendency to want to make something we do over and over again, easier, simpler and more efficient. And that's what happened. The work became more natural, beautiful, and effective. I shaped myself to it and it to me in a kind of developmental dance.

I want to make a kind of analogy between doing Hakomi and playing music. There are skills that need to be mastered in both disciplines. The reason musicians practice so much is so that they don't have to think about what notes to play. They immediately translate either something in their mind or something on paper into physical, musical expression. And once that skill is completely habitual, once you don't have to think of what notes to play, because all that is done at an unconscious level, then you can relate to the music with your personality and your feelings. You don't have to concentrate on what the notes are.

There's something similarly true about Hakomi. There are skills, skills that have to become habitual. When you know the techniques and the method at an unconscious level, you can meet the client in a new way. More intimate. More direct and connected. When your skills are highly developed, you're don't become distracted by your own thinking. You can be very present when you don't have to think.

Another analogy I'd like to make is this: great musicians make their playing look almost magical. It looks so easy and so simple when they play. It seems effortless. Good therapy also feels effortless. Having done this work for forty years, around three hours a day on average, I have learned a lot of things that are now handled by my unconscious mind. If asked, I can usually go back and explain why I did something, but at the time I did it, I wasn't consciously thinking about it. At the moment I did it, I just did it. I can remember doing a workshop at Esalen 10-15 years ago. At the very end, when people said how much they liked it, I realized I felt like I hadn't really done anything. I felt like it just happened.

In a way, after forty years of practice, the work became much simpler. Not just because the skills had matured, but because, as Picasso once put it, 'art is the elimination of the unnecessary'. I learned to eliminate what wasn't necessary.

In that forty-year process of learning my craft, I adopted many new things, but not as many as I gave up. As a result, the work has become simple for me.

The thing that has been on my mind lately is matching psychotherapy to our inherited human capacities. A book that talks about inherited capacities is called "Gut Feelings" by Gerd Gigerenzer. For example, in humans, the capacity for language is inherited; we're born with the capacity to learn a language. However, which language you learn depends on where you're born and the language of your family and society. We're born with the capacity, but it's experience that shapes our capabilities. I want to look at the inherited capacities that are most important for becoming a psychotherapist.

Offering comfort to someone we care for is an inherited human capacity. It's a capacity that needs to be developed into a capability because it is essential to the work we do. It's built into the method from start to finish, from loving presence to the healing process.

Another capacity we need to develop as Hakomi practitioners is understanding non-verbal signals and signs. A therapist needs to understand facial expressions and tone of voice. We're born with a brain that has evolved for these purposes. When those parts of our brains don't develop into capabilities, we don't develop socially. We do not develop what Stephen Porges calls the social engagement system, at least not a well functioning one.

Another inherent capacity to develop is the ability to understand the mind of another – what I call modeling. Rebecca Saxe is a cognitive neuroscientist at the Saxelab at MIT. She studies how we think about other people's thoughts by using fMRI to identify what happens in our brains when we consider the motives, passions and beliefs of others. (see Saxe 2009)

Loving Presence

I added that about fifteen years ago. Loving presence is the ideal state of mind for the therapist. It sets the general tone of the relationship. It's very significant. I talked recently about the great mistakes of the Western World. I thought one of the great mistakes was the notion that we are separate beings. That's the opposite of the Buddhist view which is: all is without a separate self. As one great scientist, Carver Mead, once said to me, "Nothing can be separated out". Our ideas about separation start with the Greeks. A wonderful book, called The Geography of Thought (Nisbett 2003) starts with the line, "The Greeks invented nature." In other words, they separated themselves from nature. They also separated themselves from each other and thought themselves independent beings. You can see this idea in its worse form in the endless killing and exploitation of humans by humans.

In quantum theory there is an amazing finding called non-locality. It says that if two molecules have interacted in the past and they separate themselves in space by say a million light years, when something happens to one of them, the other will reflect it instantaneously. Now, light can't go that fast, but non-locality is real. Such a thought cannot make sense to the ordinary Western mind. How can these two things be affecting one another instantaneously at such incredible distances. So, there is a good reason to believe that separation was a mistake.

Loving presence reflects the Buddhist position that we are not separate. If you sit with a client and feel this connection, if you feel non-separateness, (I mean feel, when the client gets sad, I can feel that sadness), if you carry that model, if you carry that way of being called loving presence, then you have created a safe and sensitive context for the work. Everything that happens, happens inside of that. And that has a tremendous effect. Loving presence by itself is healing.

The ability to be non-intrusive is a very important aspect of loving presence. You won't be loving and present when you're intrusive, when you take over and run everything. When you're running everything or asking a lot of questions, those things intrude on the client's natural process.

I love this Taoist expression: "The sage works by letting things take their natural course." That's a perfect expression of non-intrusiveness. The sage does not intrude on nature. Our tradition in the western world is just the opposite. We think we're here to conquer nature. We have that attitude. We think we can control nature. Well, you can ask yourself. How're we doing?

Loving presence has two basic qualities. You have to be radically present, which means you're not busy. To be present your attention has to be on the client. It's like keeping your hands on the wheel and your eyes on the road. No texting! So you have to be radically present. Your consciousness, your attention never leaves the client. That's one part of presence. That's how you get to follow the client's experience. You never miss anything.

The other basic thing is being loving. That's just a matter of finding something to love, appreciate, feel good about for this particular client. It's about not being absorbed in your self, not being egocentric.

Loving presence, even though the client may not consciously notice it, has a tremendous effect on the process. People know when someone is compassionate and paying attention.

The Use of Silence and Following

The use of silence is a good example of refinements I have made to Hakomi. Over the years, I began to leave more and more time for the client to simply turn inward while I waited without interrupting. For people who observe me doing sessions, that's one of the things they notice and most often comment on. It seems so obvious now, but it took me thirty years to actually understand it.

It's not only the use of silence that's important. You also have to surrender the idea that you have to always be leading and responsible. When you give that idea up, you discover that you're really there to support something positive that takes place within the client. The client has resources. If you're not intrusive, if you're not taking charge all the time and running things, you give the client respect and room to use those resources. The client isn't necessarily conscious that you're doing that, but it will have a significant effect nonetheless. It will encourage spontaneous processes to emerge. That's one key to the Refined Method; it is determined to be nonintrusive. I talk about it as following. You get in sync with the adaptive unconscious and follow its directions, the spontaneous directions it takes when you signal by your behavior that you will follow the client.

Once you've helped the client to feel safe and once you've signaled the client that you will be silent when they need you to be silent, the client will probably have something spontaneous happen. A good experiment in mindfulness will certainly do that. Reactions to experiments are best when what they evoke is surprising, unexpected and unplanned. That's the very definition of spontaneous.

Learning to focus on and work with the spontaneous was probably the most significant refinement I made to the method. It's part of a general shift that involves the state of mind of the therapist. In that, it's related to loving presence. The shift says, *Be nonintrusive! Recognize the client's healing power and the power of the adaptive unconscious!* It says, *Step back! You're only an assistant here!*

Indicators

Several years ago, I gave up thinking about character patterns. Of course I studied them a lot before that, so they are there in the back of my mind. I don't use them when I work and I don't teach them anymore. Instead of character patterns, I use and teach indicators. Indicators are external signs, shown in the client's behavior patterns, of what kind of situations and adaptations to those situations, the client may have experienced in his or her early history. The indicators suggest what core beliefs may be running the client's life.

You can spot an indicator very quickly, in a few seconds sometimes. Once I see an indicator, I usually create a guess about what it means. I'm only seeing the surface behavior, a little, personal habit. The idea is that something deeper is driving it. There are hundreds of these habits and, having worked with them for years, I usually have a good guess about what they likely will mean for clients who have them.

In Hakomi, making guesses about another's reality is called "modeling". In your mind, you're building a model of the client's history and beliefs. It's like reverse engineering: you have the product (the indicator) and you have to figure out how it was made. In this case, how it served in the client's early life situation. You have to get some ideas about the meaning in order to do an experiment. Using your guess about the meaning of the indicator, you can then create an experiment. The experiment will not only test your guess, it will, if it's a good one, move the therapy process along as no other intervention could.

I don't know when I got so curious about these little habits I call indicators. When I'm watching someone, I may notice a habit they have or a quality they have. The habit may appear as often as four or five times in the first minute. In the early part of a session, nervousness might not be an indicator, but it still could be something to work with. However, if it comes up frequently in the course of ordinary conversation, it may be something to think about and work with.

A little habit that is expressed frequently, automatically, without conscious deliberation, is an indicator. Another kind of indicator is what I'd call "a quality". Imagine someone who seems to be very contained, not expressing anything with any intensity. The person's movements are small. The person's voice is quiet. We could say the person has a habit of containing expression - that's an indicator.

There's yet another source of indicators. It's what they're doing when they're not doing anything. An article in Science (Mason et al, 2007) refers to the brain's default mode. In the study, scientists recorded peoples' brainwaves. When people focusing, not busy with any task, not relating to anyone, they have a habit of going into a particular brain state referred to as the default mode. If you notice someone whose brain is in its default mode, there is a quality to what the person is like. And that's an indicator.

These are the kinds of things you're looking and listening for: habits, qualities, default modes. You are observing, noticing, what this

Refinements

person looks like, sounds like, moves like. What kind of gestures do they make? What kind of facial expression do they have when they're not relating to anyone, when they're not doing anything exactly in particular?

Some indicators are only small parts of larger patterns of behavior. The indicators are simply external expressions of beliefs and adaptations which have become the person's way of perceiving and being in the world. Indicators are the tip of the iceberg of the self.

The habits and qualities we can notice are the surface expressions of the adaptive behaviors developed to handle situations and emotions experienced in life, usually early in life.

Indicators are automatic. People don't do them deliberately or consciously. I'll give you a few examples. There are people who end almost every sentence with a question mark. Now if they're Canadians that's normal. For Canadians, it seems to be a cultural habit of seeking agreement. In Americans, it usually means something else. What I've often found is that there are two possible underlying questions that are being asked. One is about being understood, perhaps a history of not expecting to be listened to or understood. The question implied by the interrogatory sound at the end of a statement is asking the question, "Do you understand me?" People who hear this typically respond with a nod or a 'yeah' in an equally automatic fashion.

Sometimes there's a much deeper question being asked. The person is, again unconsciously asking, "Is it okay that I'm here?" "Is it okay that I exist." That's a serious situation. It's about being wanted, being welcomed in the world or into the world, if it goes that far back. Something like that could be signaling something traumatic or close to it.

Another common, easy to understand indicator is shrugging of the shoulders. It's usually saying something like, "I'm not responsible." "I don't know." "It's not my fault." Here is an example. You ask a friend, "How did you like the movie?" Your friend replies, "I liked the movie." But when she says that, she also shrugs her shoulders. You can bet she didn't like the movie that much. For me, this indicator talks about a habit of avoiding responsibility and the history is probably about blame and being made to feel guilty. That's my guess, based on a lot of experience working with this indicator.

Another common indicator is for a person not to look at you straight on. They turn their heads a little left or right and look at you from an angle. They can turn the head and sometimes tilt it slightly. You can do several kinds of experiments with any of those indicators.

Another common indicator is self touching. There are a lot of ways clients do that in therapy sessions. They rub their hands. They stroke their chins or rub their legs. Those indicators are about comforting, needing touch to calm down. If you work with it, one thing you can do is have an assistant take it over. When the touching is taken over, you can ask the client, "What does that hand seem to be saying to you?" Like most kinds of touch, self-touching is meaningful - it's not just a physical sensation.

There are hundreds of indicators. Many are written on the face. The default facial expression is probably the easiest to detect. It should be easy to get an idea about what the belief is or how the habit is serving the person by noticing what the person's face looks like when the person isn't relating to anyone else. What is the default mode face? What is the facial expression when there are no faces around to worry about? What is the expression when doing nothing?

There's an indicator you don't want to work with at all. When a person has a habit of closing his eyes and/or looking away while being silent, it usually means the person is thinking or remembering. That indicator tells you that the person needs some time to herself and doesn't want to be disturbed. So, wait patiently until she opens her eyes, looks at you and starts talking.

There's another kind of facial expression that isn't an indicator. They are what are called micro expressions and they have been written about extensively by Paul Ekman (2003). Micro expressions are micro because they go by very quickly. They're about momentary activities and experiences. Indicators are long-term. They talk about personality and development.

I don't use indicators to make diagnoses - I use them to design experiments. When I discover an indicator, it's going to suggest two kinds of things to me. First of all, it's going to suggest something about the client's way of dealing with the world and the core beliefs that are shaping that. Secondly, it's going to suggest the situation or situations that made that way of dealing with the world necessary and successful. I do a kind of reverse engineering. I ask myself, how does this habit serve this person? What kind of situation would this have been useful in? I think of it as an adaptation to some kind of situation, some kind of pressure. So, I'm asking myself, what is the source of this thing? And I call that part of the method modeling or getting meaning. I used to ask clients questions in order to get meanings. Now, I just think about it. Clients don't always consciously know the sources of their behaviors.

Indicators are data, observations to hypothesize about. You have to have an experimental attitude, think like a scientist. Given this data, what might explain it? Like any scientist, you have to make guesses about what will explain your observations, your data. In your mind, you ponder, why does this person have this quality? How did it arise in this person's life? If you get a good idea, you do an experiment to test it. You can train yourself to think that way. This is the scientific method and how science works. It looks at some data and asks what kind of theory explains this data? And not only do scientists want to explain the data, they want to test their theories.

Experiments

The unique contribution of the Hakomi method is this: the method contains, as a necessary element, precise experiments done with the client in a mindful state, the purpose being to evoke emotions, memories and reactions that will reveal or help access the beliefs, experiences and adaptations that are influencing the person's habitual behaviors.

From the indicator, I get some ideas about beliefs and history, and from those, I decide what experiments I could do to test my ideas. A good experiment has a chance of evoking a healing process. Experiments are designed to evoke reactions. We want to say something or do something that evokes something unexpected and something that touches the client's core beliefs. We want to invite old, painful memories into consciousness, so we can replay those memories and put a new ending to them. We want to bring core beliefs into consciousness so they can be changed. So, we do something that creates consciousness around them.

Given the safety created by loving presence, during and after an experiment, a client may be in a very open state of mind. Access to feelings, images, and memories of intense experiences is much easier in that state and the reaction to an experiment can easily be the beginning of a healing process. The signs that something like that is happening are: emotions arising, a spontaneous sense of tension or impulse to move, an image or an emotionally charged memory arises. The experiment and the client's willingness to allow reactions have accessed this unconscious material. It's material that's probably been kept unconscious because it is associated with events that couldn't be managed at the time the events occurred. Most likely, adaptations were created to deal with the situation, adaptations that avoid having to feel the pain that was part of those events. Once the painful memories or feelings are back in consciousness, you can help the person heal.

We do our experiments with our client in a mindful state. Mindfulness is a calm, sensitive state, in which the client is focused on his or her own present experience. The client will be quite able to notice any reaction to the experiment. If your experiment evokes a reaction, the client will be very likely to notice it.

What kinds of experiments do we want to create? First of all, we want to test our guesses. That's true of all experiments. But for us, there is another purpose, a deeper purpose. We want to evoke a healing process. To do that, we have to bring something that needs healing into consciousness.

A good experiment causes the client's expectations to fail. We try to offer experiments that don't fit the client's model of the world and thereby create consciousness. Since we look for indicators that reflect the client's adaptations to emotionally painful experiences, those painful experiences and feelings come into consciousness. When they do, you have the beginning of a healing process.

There is a wonderful book called *On Intelligence* by a man named Jeff Hawkins (2004). He is both an electronic designer and a

Refinements

neurologist, designed the Palm and the Trio and runs an institute where people study the neocortex. In his book, he describes what the neocortex is doing in a theory he calls the Memory Prediction Framework.

The Memory Prediction Framework postulates that the neocortex records our experiences. It remembers them and it remembers what followed them. It remembers sequences. When a present experience is happening and it's similar to one of the remembered ones, the neocortex makes a prediction about what will follow the new experience. It automatically predicts what going to happen next. Hawkins, in one of his talks, gives this example: "Everyone in this room knows exactly how I am going to end this...." and he stops right there. What happens is that, for almost everyone, the word "sentence" just pops into their heads. They predicted it. They predict the word "sentence" because that's just what ought to follow, what always has followed similar sentences in the past.

Hawkins says that's how the brain works. Hawkins also gives examples of what happens when an automatic prediction fails. Here's his example: If, while we are here, a carpenter goes to your house moves the front door knob an inch away from where it has always been. When you go home, what's going to happen? You know that doorknob and where it has been located on your door for twenty-five years. You do not have to consciously think about where the doorknob is. Your neocortex, with all those years of experiences, can handle the situation without troubling you to pay much attention. You could be totally thinking about something else. You're going to reach for the doorknob using the memory of where it's always been. Your brain has predicted it's going to be there, but, when you reach for it, it's not where you predicted. What happens is you're surprised. You're suddenly conscious of something being different, something you didn't expect. Your prediction has failed and now you are conscious.

You weren't conscious of your prediction before it failed. You would have just reached for the doorknob out of habit. You wouldn't need to think about it. That's what habits are for, they're time savers. They conserve consciousness so it can handle thinks that need thinking about.

We design experiments that will make the client's predictions fail. If the indicator suggests that the client is going to expect (predict) blame, when the client is mindful and ready, I'm going to say, "Please notice what happens when I tell you, 'It's not your fault'". That's the experiment I'm going to do. "It's not your fault." And if I'm right, the client's blame doorknob is not going to be where they thought it was. Metaphorically, my experiment will crash right into what the client's belief system will be predicting. If they expect blame and I tell them it's not their fault, I should get a reaction. That's the design. That's the very core of the method. Make guesses and create experiments that make prediction fail.

The Healing Process

The goal of Hakomi is to evoke and support a healing process and healing is a spontaneous process. It proceeds and is directed from within the client. If your experiment works, feelings and/or memories are evoked. That's the best outcome for an experiment because it tells you that you've touched something important. What happens next? What I do now is different from what I did before. It's another way the method has become simpler. Once an experiment evokes an emotional reaction, let's say sadness, there are two things to do. One of those things is to remain silent! The reason is that once an emotion is felt, an automatic process follows in which the mind tries to make sense of the emotion. If a client starts to feel something like sadness, the client's mind will search for associations. If you don't interrupt the process, a memory might arise or a thought. You can make a short contact statement, like "Some sadness". If you start asking questions like, "Why are you so sad?" or worse, "Where do you feel that in your body?" you will be intruding on a natural, spontaneous process and you will take the client out of that process and into answering questions and giving explanations.

I used to do this sort of thing. I called it deepening. It was supposed to help the client stay with his or her experience. I have learned that clients will usually do that automatically if you don't interfere. So, nowadays, I stay silent, especially if the client closes his

Refinements

or her eyes and stays silent also. For me, that's a sign that the client is doing inner work and that's the beginning of the healing process.

I'll give you some simple signs that tell you to be silent:
- When a client closes her eyes, and looks like she's thinking, be silent and wait!
- And, when the client opens his eyes and looks at you, also wait! Leave room for the client to organize his thoughts and then, leave room for the client to tell you those thoughts. When a client's been inside for a while and comes back out and looks at me, I will be there looking at them and waiting to hear what they have to tell me. That's important. The client needs to know that I am interested and paying attention. The client doesn't have to think about it, but at some level, the client realizes it. And if you're there waiting, patiently, attentively, the client will tell you what happened when he was inside and had their eyes closed.
- Another very important time to be silent is when someone begins to feel emotional, it's okay to make a contact statement, but don't intrude. Let the process develop without trying to run it.

These simple things are a great way to build relationships.

Healing is a spontaneous process. Clients don't need to give you explanations, and you don't need to give them explanations. There are ways to follow and support the healing process, once you've recognized it has started. When you follow and support the spontaneous unfolding of the healing process then deep healing can happen. It may take minutes, hours or days, but it can happen. There are some guidelines for doing this.

Offer and give comfort. Touch and hold your client, if they give permission and respond with relief or the continued release of emotion. One of the saddest things about psychotherapy in the U.S. is the legal issue that surrounds touching clients. That idea is absurd and obscene. Comfort is what we humans offer and use when someone is feeling pain. We need it then. Even animals do it. Our primate buddies do it, chimps, bonobos, gorillas. Dogs do it. Bears. Mammals. Our fellow mammals comfort each other. It's an inherited capacity in every one of those species.

After an experiment, when you notice signs, even subtle ones, that the client is becoming sad, you offer to touch the person, you offer to put a hand on her shoulder or her arm. Before you do that, you check to see if it's okay with her. You ask her or you just notice the nonverbal head nods and facial expressions that signal her permission. When you do put your hand on the client, you don't start talking or asking questions! You remain silent, calm and silent. You wait. She may want to talk or she may simply close her eyes and go inside to be with her unfolding experience.

Once the healing process starts and continues to be supported, it will unfold spontaneously. After your client has been inside awhile, something new emerges. She opens her eyes and looks at you. You wait, looking back at her and she begins to tell you about her experience. A long-buried, painful memory comes into consciousness. As she tells you about this, a new wave of feeling comes over her. Her feelings are deeper now. You offer to hold her. She accepts and comes into your arms and really begins to sob. Again, you don't say anything for a while. You simply hold her. Then gently, you offer some comforting words. The process is fully underway now. You've done the right things to support it and you haven't done anything that would have interrupted the process, like asking questions or starting a conversation.

The Use of Assistants

Another thing I introduced into the refined method was the use of assistants. They assist when a client experiences a painful emotion as an outcome of an experiment. They offer comfort. If it's accepted, they provide it. Sometimes it is just a hand on the client's arm or shoulder. Sometimes it's being held in someone's arms for a while. When my assistants offer touch or holding, like me, they remain silent. Either way, it's never done without acceptance and it's done in silence.

Refinements

I've been asked many, many times how to do this without assistants. Well, I don't know; I rarely face that situation. I always have at least one assistant. If I can't muster some regular assistants, I'll ask the client to bring some. Sometimes, very rarely, I work one on one, but I much prefer using assistants. Assistants can help contain the process when strong emotions are being expressed. With assistants, there is a semi-public aspect to the therapy. The process is being witnessed. It is not just therapist and client. It's happening in a group of some size, from three or four to a whole workshop full of people. That has a powerful affect on the client mind. You have told your story and others have heard it. Sympathetic people know your story.

> From a paper dated 2010 called Hakomi Simplified: The Refined Method

Hakomi Simplified

"Make everything as simple as possible, but not simpler." (Einstein)

"Beauty is a very successful criterion for choosing the right theory, a beautiful or elegant theory is more likely to be right than a theory that is inelegant. Why on earth could that be so?"
(Murray Gell-Mann, 2007)

"Art is the elimination of the unnecessary."
(Picasso)

My work is very simple. It just took me forty years to make it so. Now I think it's as simple as it's going to get. I did a lot of reading and thinking during those forty years. I made a lot of changes. For the first ten years I had a private practice. I started with Gestalt and later moved on to Bioenergetics. My love of Taoism and Buddhism started ten years before that. By the time I left private practice and started teaching, my work had become a complete method. It contained some defining unique elements. In 1981, during one of the first trainings, I named it, The Hakomi Method. Right after that first training, I founded the Hakomi Institute.

As the Institute grew, the method also grew. New techniques and theory were added. Handbooks were written. The work becoming complex. Graphics were produced, lists drawn up. Lots of writing, too! Dozens of new experiential exercises were created. Most of these developments were covered in my book, Body Centered Psychotherapy: The Hakomi Method, published in 1990. All along, a large body of scientific literature influenced the changes I was making to the method.

You might expect that the method would have just kept getting more complex. It didn't happen that way. Years of teaching and doing therapy helped me understand what was actually necessary and what wasn't. The growing scientific literature was full of discoveries and ideas that made sense of what I was trying to do as a therapist. They helped me boil down my understanding of the method to a few general truths. Rudolpho Llinás influenced me when he described the brain as a virtual reality machine. (Llinás 2002) Jonah Lehrer's (2007) idea that every memory is inseparable from the moment of its recollection influenced me.

I was blessed with several kinds of support that are rare for a psychotherapist. For example, I did dozens of therapy sessions as demonstrations in the classes I was teaching. I made videos of those sessions. I went over those videos with others. I got lots of feedback. In class, I saw how the people responded to the demos. I was always ready to change things if I saw a better way. I was the creator of the method and I never stopped creating. Year by year, I learned more and more what helped and what was harmful or unnecessary. The result was that the method became simple. Much simpler that it had been. Slowly, over a decade or more, I have refined it.

This new simplified method is the very best way I know to support a person's mental-emotional healing. Being simple, the method does not interfere. Being simple, it is graceful and efficient. Being simple, it acts in accordance with nature. The new method offers deep kindness, true presence and the skills to help without forcing anything.

What follows is a description of the basic elements of the refined version of Hakomi.

Ten Basic Elements of the Refined Method

1. Focus on Present Experience

Kahneman (2012) refers to two selves, an experiencing self and a remembering self. The theory postulates a self that is having experiences which are changing from moment to moment and another self that remembers those experiences. The experiencing self is, to some degree, capable of what he calls reliving an experience. He also calls this "re-experiencing". Here's how Kahneman describes the two selves:

> "...we might be thinking of ourselves and of other people in terms of two selves. There is an experiencing self, who lives in the present and knows the present is capable of re-living the past, but basically it has only the present. It's the experiencing self that the doctor approaches—you know, when the doctor asks, "Does it hurt now when I touch you here?" And then there is a remembering self, and the remembering self is the one that keeps score, and maintains the story of our life, and it's the one that the doctor approaches in asking the question, "How have you been feeling lately?" or "How was your trip to Albania?" or something like that. Those are two very different entities, the experiencing self and the remembering self and getting confused between them is part of the mess of the notion of happiness.
>
> Now, the remembering self is a storyteller. And that really starts with a basic response of our memories—it starts immediately. We don't only tell stories when we set out to tell stories. Our memory tells us stories, that is, what we get to keep from our experiences is a story."

Thinking in terms of two selves is one of the theoretical foundations of the refined method and a very practical one at that. First of all, the method requires that the therapist be constantly paying attention to what her client is experiencing. A client's present moment experience

Refinements

is how the therapist gets the information she needs to support the unfolding process. The therapist's primary relationship is with the experiencing self. She is "in conversation" with it continuously.

For example, when I'm working, I stay aware of what my client is experiencing and I respond to it. I am continuously relating to the experiencing self. There are clear signs if you pay attention to them. In the trainings we teach students to attend to those signs and to respond to them, sometimes with a contact statement, sometimes with silence. Sometimes it signals that the healing phase has begun or that it's ended. What we do and when we do it depends on what our client is experiencing at that moment. This is one way we show our respect for the client's healing power.

We're also paying attention to the remembering self, especially when a painful memory arises and the client is re-living a painful experience. So, we listen to the remembering self and we watch for memories or pieces of memories that have a chance of morphing into a healing process. But we're not having the usual kind of conversation about the past that one might have in a "non-therapeutic" setting. It's not just questions and answers. We're not asking for a story about what happened. It's not that kind of conversation. The "real" conversation is what's happening between what the client is experiencing and what we do in response to that.

Another defining aspect of the refined method involves the experiencing self and what constitutes healing.

2. Healing and Reconsolidation

"Okay, in therapy you build a new memory. But how do you change neural networks that may have original templates that are not so positive?" His answer was, "When there is an affective tag attached to a known experience you create a new memory." (Bruce Perry 2007)

"Ample evidence suggests that upon their retrieval, items in long-term memory enter a transient special state, in which they might become prone to change. The process that generates this state is dubbed 'reconsolidation." (Yadin Dudai 2006)

The refined method works with a certain kind of problem that client's have: certain positive, emotionally nourishing experiences are not available to them. The reason for this involves powerful, usually early, painful experiences that have left clients with adaptations that avoid any repetition of those painful experiences. In avoiding those experiences, related positive experiences are also avoided. Clients have ingrained habits and over-generalized beliefs that protect them from whole classes of experiences, both painful and nourishing. For example: If you have been abandoned by a parent, you will avoid that kind of outcome by not becoming so attached to anyone again. By avoiding that, you'll never have the deep satisfaction and pleasure of belonging or being in love.

Our goal in therapy is to help clients learn that they don't always have to avoid the things they've been avoiding, that their beliefs are over-generalized, that their habits keep them from emotional nourishment that's available, if they can differentiate. Clients have implicit beliefs like, "I'm not lovable." They have habits as a result of the experiences that brought them to that belief. As a result, they cannot see the love that's available to them. We help them realize that. We help them become able to have certain emotionally nourishing experiences that they've been missing due to the beliefs and habits they attained though the painful experiences of their early life.

We help clients expand their experiencing self's possibilities to include the nourishing experiences they've been missing. Our method is simple. We evoke the re-experiencing of those early painful memories and, during a period of reconsolidation, we supply emotionally positive affective tags to create a new memory and new beliefs about what's possible for the client. The tags we attach are these: caring, comforting words, voice and touch, our calm presence, our faith in the outcome and a healthy, relaxed sense of humor. These are the affective tags that create the new memory. The process is called reconsolidation. The final outcome of therapy is not just a new memory, it's a new capacity to experience.

3. Loving Presence

The creation of the healing relationship requires that the therapist be a certain kind of person, a person who is naturally compassionate, able to be radically present, able to give full attention to another, able to see deeply into people and to understand what is seen.

Loving presence as a basic element was added to the refined method in 1987. This is about the therapist's state of mind and the effect these have on the client. The therapist brings himself into a loving state by looking for and finding something about the client that inspires caring and appreciation. Being in this state primes the client's sense of safety, a necessary aspect of moving into painful memories and feelings. Many cues about the therapist are taken in outside of the client's consciousness. These have a strong effect on how the client experiences being and reacts to being in the therapeutic relationship. The therapist's personality is, of course, the most important aspect of the setting in which therapy takes place. (see Mahoney 1992)

The therapist is also present—radically present—in the sense that he or she is continuously attending to the client's present experience. Staying present this way is called tracking. Tracking was part of the original version of the method and remains a part of the new, refined version. Making contact statements and following the client's spontaneous behaviors rely on this kind of radical presence.

4. The Right Use of Silence

There are times during a therapy sessions when clients need the therapist to be silent. A good sense of when that is, is another new element making up the refined method. Silence signals the client that the therapist is in touch and will honor what the client needs in terms of time. Silence allows the client time to think, to remember, to feel and to find the next thing that wants to happen. It also helps, when the time comes, for the client to integrate and reconsolidate the new experience. We support the client's process at times like those simply by not intruding. Here's what Salvador Minuchin had to say about intruding:

> *"As a physician I was trained to take over, to become a leader, and to take responsibility. As a therapist I also had to learn the language of silence, to learn how to become invisible, to learn how not*

> *to intrude and at the same time, to be central. Achieving a centrality that can get people's attention without being so intrusive that you take too much responsibility, is essential in the process of therapy."*   - Salvador Minuchin (2009)

This is another element that makes the method experiential. The pace is different. We're not engaged in a conversation; that is, we're not simply exchanging words. We're interacting with another's present experience. We're recognizing what the other needs from us at the moment. And one big thing that's needed is time to do one's inner work, the work of remembering and thinking and feeling. This kind of aware responding is rare in ordinary conversation and often in ordinary psychotherapy. In ordinary conversation, ideas are exchanged. Questions are asked and answered. The remembering self handles most of that. In the refined method, we want something very different. We want a "conversation" with the experiencing self.

If you can recognize the client's need for silence and respond to it early in a session, the relationship and the process will take on a different character from ordinary conversation. The client will be primed to take her time. She will not have to split her attention between what she's experiencing and having to respond to ordinary conversation. A different level of intimacy results when silence is used. Whether the client is conscious of it or not, a sense of respect and caring is felt. That's very important.

The simple signs of the need for silence are these: the client closes her eyes and doesn't speak for a while. Sometimes the client looks away for a few moments. These simple signs suggests the need for silence. Simple signs; simple response. When we honor the need for silence, we honor the experiencing self. Something in client, call it the adaptive unconscious (Wilson, 2002), will begin to trust you and help you as the process unfolds.

5. Indicators and Modeling

There are minor habits—like shrugging one's shoulders or looking askance at people—that are subtle, present day expressions of events that may have happened long ago. They are small pieces of remembered experiences, sometimes painful experiences that we learned to avoid. I call that kind of habit, an indicator. There are hundreds of them. We can think of them as external expressions of the adaptive unconscious. Being habitual, they are not consciously planned behaviors. At best, they act at the edges of consciousness, if they're conscious at all. And, they provide a clear, easy way to bring those old, painful experiences into consciousness.

An indicator is a "quality", as in, *Not even the thousand eyes of five hundred Buddhas could discern in him, any particular quality.* That's an old Zen way of saying, he's empty or "no indicators". An indicator might be something an author would use to describe a character she's writing about or an actor to depict a character.

The way we use an indicator once we've found it is to create an experiment intended to evoke a reaction. We want to bring some aspect of the painful memory into consciousness. Experiments are described in detail elsewhere. As part of creating an experiment, we may think about what sort of history or beliefs might be associated with it. We want some ideas about the meaning of the indicator. We make some guesses about, "what kind of experience created the need for this kind of indicator?" "How is this habit serving the client?" "What beliefs might be associated with the behavior" That kind of thinking is called modeling. Experiments not only evoke reactions, they test the models we've guessed. Creating and implementing experiments was also part of the original version of the method, though modeling wasn't taught as such.

6. Precise Experiments in Mindfulness

The unique contribution of the Hakomi method is this: the method contains, as a necessary element, precise experiments done with the client in a mindful state, the purpose being to evoke emotions, memories and reactions that will reveal or help access the beliefs, experiences and adaptations that are influencing the person's habitual behaviors. These evoked reactions initiate the healing phase of the process.

7. Becoming Conscious

Hawkin's Memory-Prediction Framework (2004): One of the more important new ideas in neurology is Hawkin's idea about the general function of the human cortex. "We experience the world as a sequence of patterns, and we store them, and we recall them. And when we recall them, we match them up against reality. We're making predictions all the time. (Hawkins 2004) Hawkins' central concept is this memory-prediction framework. It states that the neocortex matches sensory inputs to stored memory patterns and this process leads to predictions of what will happen in the immediate future when a pattern occurs. For example, if I start saying "a, b, c, d", you'll automatically predict that "e" will be the next thing I'll say. You predict that because you know the sequence. It's stored in your cortex. It will be so obvious to you, you will not even notice that you're predicting. You would notice if I said, "a, b, c, d, m". That's not the sequence you remember and it's not what you'd expect to come next. Something's not quite right. So, you start paying attention. The general idea is this: when an event does not fit our unconscious prediction, we notice it, meaning: we become conscious.

Here's how this fits. Our experiments with clients are designed to make the client's predictions fail and that evokes a reaction. The kind of predictions we seek to make fail are the ones we have modeled from the client's indicators. If we model the angle of the head, for instance, we might think it's telling us about an historical need to be cautious. So, our experiment might be to say to the client (while she's in a mindful state) "You can trust me." What that verbal experiment might do is evoke a sense of disbelief and possibly a slight feeling of fear. That sense and that feeling are pieces of the old painful memory and can be used to bring it into consciousness. Once these appear, the healing phase is beginning. There are ways to then support its natural unfolding. If the re-experiencing becomes intense enough, and the right support is given, then reconsolidation can happen and will have a powerful healing effect.

Refinements

8. Following the Healing Process

In practicing "following", be aware of the client's spontaneous behavior and when you notice it, do something with it. If a client tells you that something just popped into her head, an image or a memory or an impulse, do something with it. Create an experiment around it. Even if you have to drop something else that you were doing, go with what comes up for the client. That's following.

I think of these spontaneous behaviors as pointing to where the process might possibly be going, as signals from the unconscious, leading us in a particular direction. It is the client's unconscious that we're following. Think of it as something the client's unconscious is telling us. We pay attention. Somewhere inside, the client knows what's needed. If the setting is right, if the relationship is right, then when a spontaneous gesture, impulse or memory arises, it is probably the adaptive unconscious moving the process towards healing. When you respond to that, you are supporting the healing process. As the old Taoist saying goes, "the sage works by letting things take their natural course." Following is taking the natural course. That makes for less effort and better results.

9. Reconsolidation using Comforting Touch, Assistants and Humor

"Every memory is inseparable from the moment of its recollection." (Lehrer, 2007)

"....what we get to keep from our experiences is a story." (Kahneman, 2010)

Healing involves changing our clients' memories. We help them change their stories about old, painful, formative experiences, experiences that shaped the client's way of being in the world. Healing changes the meaning of those experiences. It changes how the story ends. Once we've evoke a re-living of those experiences, we provide comforting touch, soothing words, and sometimes fun and laughter. A whole new ending is being attached to the story. The old beliefs no longer hold. A new way of being becomes possible. That's how reconsolidation works and how it's part of the refined method.

In effect, we help clients recover the capacity to experience emotionally nourishing experiences that were previously avoided. We help them try out new beliefs and new behaviors.

When painful memories arise, I have an assistant or two comfort the client by gently touching the client on the shoulder or back. If the client goes deeper into the memory, feeling it more intensely and expressing those feelings, I have my assistants hold her as you would anyone in need of comforting. The effect is reconsolidation. The memory is changed. Recall that, "every memory is inseparable from the moment of its recollection." The client's moments of recollection are filled with care and comforting. This alters the memory and its influence on the client's subsequent beliefs, thoughts and feelings. While this is happening, we remain silent, giving the client time to experience the spontaneous insights and integration that generally accompany a period of reconsolidation.

As noted, I use assistants. This is an essential part of the Refined Method. I typically use one or two assistants. I use them to help with the experiments and during the healing process. If I'm working before a whole group, I may even use the group as a "Greek chorus". Usually, my assistants are people I have trained, though I sometimes have people from the group assist. The setting is usually a workshop or training that I'm leading. When I do a private session, I also have assistants. I'll arrange to have some of my students there or I'll ask the client to bring a friend or a spouse. There are two big advantages to using assistants. Touch is much safer in a group setting. More importantly, it provides a special kind of support and the physical expression of caring.

One last thing about reconsolidation: humor can be as powerful as comforting. Laughter and fun are very different endings to remembered pain.

10. Deliberate Practice and Myelination

Fritz Perls once said, "Learning is the discovery of the possible." That's one of the things that happens in a successful therapy session. The client discovers that something that's been missing, something wanted and heartwarming has become possible. The client experiences its reality. The possibility of love, of safety, of the freedom to express, some lovely new feeling and understanding happens. But, what happens in a session is only the beginning. Long-term change requires repetition. It requires practice. A fresh new set of beliefs, actions and experiences will have to be enacted repeatedly, in the course of the client's everyday living. Permanent change takes practice, and the best kind of practice is what I call "deliberate practice".

Deliberate practice is the mechanism by which the neural circuits are strengthened, made to work quicker and automatically. Neurologically, it is the building of myelin around nerve networks through repeated use. The process is described beautifully in Daniel Coyle's book, *The Talent Code* (2009). Deliberate practice is practicing at the edge of one's skill level. It's going over and over the actions needed to become better at whatever it is you're doing. Some of this habit building goes on in a therapy session, as much as is possible given the time constraints.

Realistically, clients have to do the bulk of their practicing outside of the therapy session. We can encourage that. We can offer ideas about how to do it but that part of the healing is mostly out of our hands. What happens in therapy illuminates a possibility, gives a taste of it, and points to what needs practice. Clients need to act on their new beliefs and repeat the new experiences out in the world, usually in situations that are somewhat challenging at first. Success requires courage and persistence. And of course support from the environment and good-hearted people.

With deliberate practice, the new behaviors become habits. The behaviors become effortless and automatic. The experiencing self now finds more experiences of happiness and confidence in the ordinary acts of simple, daily living. And that, in the final analysis, is what the method helps make happen.

Bibliography

Bibliography

Almaas, A.H. *"The Optimizing Thrust of Being"* http://www.ahalmaas.com/glossary/luminosity/4802 (A.H. Almaas is the pen name of A. Hameed Ali (born 1944), an author and spiritual teacher who writes about and teaches an approach to spiritual development informed by modern psychology and therapy which he calls the Diamond Approach.)

Allport, G. *The Nature of Prejudice*. Addison-Weley Publishing, 1954.

Bargh, J.A. and Chartrand T.L. *The Unbearable Automaticity of Being*. American Psychologist 54(7), 462-479. July 1999.

Bhante Henepola Gunaratana *Mindfulness in Plain English*. Wisdom Publications, 2011.

Blakeslee, S., Ramachandran, V.S. *Phantoms in the Brain*. Avon, 1999.

Brenman-Gibson, M. *Worlds in Harmony: Dialogs on Compassionate Action*. H. H. Dalai Lama, Berkeley, CA: Parallax Press, 1992.

Bromberg, Philip M. *Standing in the Spaces: Essays on Clinical Process, Trauma and Dissociation*. Hillsdale, NJ: The Analytic Press, 1998.

Bromberg, Philip M. *Awakening the Dreamer: Clinical Journeys*. Mahwah, NJ: The Analytic Press, 2006.

Brooks, D. *"Lost in the Crowd."* The New York Times, 16 Dec, 2008.

Brooks, D. *"Genius: The Modern View."* The New York Times, 1 May, 2009.

Calvin, William H. *How Brains Think: Evolving Intelligence, Then and Now*. New York: Basic Books, 1996.

Calvin, William H. *Ephemeral Levels of Mental Organization: Darwinian Competitions as a Basis for Consciousness*. Seattle: University of Washington, 1998.

Bibliography

Calvin, William. *Lingua Ex Machine: Reconciling Darwin and Chomsky with the Human Brain*. Bradford Books. MIT Press, 2000.

Carey, Benedict (July 31, 2007) *"Who's Minding the Mind?"* The New York Times Company, http://www.nytimes.com/2007/07/31/health/psychology/31subl.html

Cassidy, J. (Ed.) and Shaver, P. R. *Handbook of Attachment: Theory, Research, and Clinical Applications*. New York: The Guilford Press, 1999.

Coyle, Daniel. *The Talent Code: Greatness Isn't Born. It's Grown. Here's How*. NY: Bantam Dell, 2009.

Crick, F. and Koch, C. *"Are we aware of neural activity in the primary visual cortex?"* Nature, Nature Publishing Group, 1995.

Damasio, A. *Descartes' Error: Emotion, Reason, and the Human Brain*. G.P. Putnam's Sons, 1994.

Damasio , A. *Looking for Spinoza: Joy, Sorrow, and the Feeling Brain*. New York: Houghton Mifflin, 2003.

De Waal, Frans. *The Age of Empathy: Nature's Lessons for a Kinder Society*. New York: Crown Publishing Group, 2009.

Depraz, N., Varela, F. J., Vermersch, P. In M.Velmans (Ed.), *Investigating Phenomenal Consciousness*. Amsterdam: John Benjamins Publishing Company, 1999.

Diamond, J. Guns, *Germs, and Steel: The Fates of Human Societies*. W.W. Norton & Company, 1997.

Dörner R., Dietrich. *The Logic of Failure: Recognizing and Avoiding Error in Complex Situation*. New York: Metropolitan Books, 1996.

Dudai, Yadin. *"Reconsolidation: The Advantage of Being Refocused."* 2006. https://www.weizmann.ac.il/neurobiology/labs/dudai/uploads/files/Dudai2006.pdf

Duddy, Thomas. *Mind, Self and Interiority*. NY: Ashgate, 1995.

Duncan, B., Miller S., Wampold, B., and Hubble, M. *The Heart & Soul of Change: Delivering What Works in Therapy.* Washington, DC: American Psychological Association, 2010.

Ekman, P. *Emotions Revealed: Recognizing Faces and Feelings to Improve Communication and Emotional Life.* Macmillan, 2003.

Edelman, G. *Bright Air, Brilliant Fire: A Nobel Laureate's Revolutionary Vision of How the Mind Originates in the Brain.* BasicBooks, 1992.

Ellenberger H. *The Discovery of the Unconscious: The History and Evolution of Synamic Psychiatry.* Basic Books, 1970.

Erickson, M. In E. Rossi (Ed.). *The collected papers of Milton H. Erickson, Section III. Utilization approaches to hypnotherapy: Vol. IV. Innovative hypnotherapy (pp. 147-234).* New York: Irvington. 1980.

Feinberg, T. E. *Altered Egos: How the Brain Creates the Self.* Oxford University Press, 2001.

Feldenkrais, M. *The Illusive Obvious.* Meta Publications, 1981.

Feynman, R. *"The Key to Science."* 1964.
https://www.youtube.com/watch?v=b240PGCMwV0

Ford, C. (1989). *Where Healing Waters Meet: Touching Mind and Emotion Through the Body.* Station Hill Press, 1992.

Frith, C. (2007) *Making Up The Mind, How the Brain Creates our Mental World.* Wiley-Blackwell, 2007.

Gawande, Atul. *"The Itch."* The New Yorker Magazine. June 30, 2008.

Gell-Mann, Murray. *"Beauty, truth and ... physics?"* Ted Talks, March 2007.

Gendlin, E. T. *"The Primacy of Human Presence: Small Steps of the Therapy Process: How They Come and How to Help Them Come."* The Gendlin Online Library, 1990
https://www.focusing.org/gendlin/docs/gol_2110.html

Gerhardt, S. *Why Love Matters: How Affection Shapes a Baby's Brain.* Brunner-Routledge, 2004.

Bibliography

Gigerenzer, G. *Gut Feelings*. Viking, 2007.

Gladwell, M. *Blink: The Power of Thinking Without Thinking*. Back Bay Books, 2005.

Gladwell, M. *Outliers: The Story of Success*. Little, Brown and Company, 2008.

Goleman, D. *Tibetan and Western Models of Mental Health,* In: H.H. Dali Lama. MindScience—An East-West Dialogue, Boston: Wisdom Publications, 1991.

Goodwin, B. *How the Leopard Changed Its Spots: The Evolution of Complexity*. Princeton University Press, 1994.

Gunaratana, B.H. *Mindfulness in Plain English: 20th Anniversary Special Edition*, Wisdom Publications, 2011.

Hall, C. S. and Nordby, V. J. *A Primer of Jungian Psychology*. Signet, 1973.

Harris, S. *The End of Faith, Religion, Terror, and the Future of Reason*. W.W. Norton and Company, 2004.

Hawkins, J. and Blakeslee, S. *On Intelligence: How a New Understanding of the Brain Will Lead to Truly Intelligent Machines*. New York: Times Books, 2004.

Herbert, M. (2000). *Incomplete Science, The Body, and Indwelling Spirit*. 15 Sept, 2000. . http://www.metanexus.net/essay/incomplete-science-body-and-indwelling-spirit.

Hilgard, E.R. *Divided Consciousness*. Wiley, 1996.

Holland, J. as cited in Waldrop, M. *Complexity: The Emerging Science at the Edge of Order and Chaos*. (pp 147) New York: Simon and Schuster, 1993.

Jaynes, J. *The Origin of Consciousness in the Breakdown of the Bicameral Mind*. Houghton Mifflin Harcourt Publishing Company, 1976.

Janet, Pierre. *The Fear of Action*. American Psychopathological Society, 1921.

Bibliography

Johnson, S. Emergence: *The Connected Lives of Ants, Brains, Cities, and Software.* Scribner, 2001.

Jung, Carl. *Psychology of the Unconscious.* 1943

Kaetz, D. Moshe Feldenkrais – *Making Connections: Hasidic Roots and Resonance in the teaching of Moshe Feldenkrais.* jMetchosin, BC: River Center Publisher, 2007.

Kahneman, D. *"The Riddle of Experience vs Memory."* Feb 2010. www.ted.com/talks/daniel_kahneman

Kahneman D. *Thinking, Fast and Slow.* Farrar, Strauss & Giroux, 2011

Kurtz, R., Prestera, H. (1976). *The Body Reveals. An Illustrated Guide to the Psychology of the Body.* Joanna Cotler Books, 1977.

Kurtz, R. *Body-Centered Psychotherapy: The Hakomi Method: The Integrated Use of Mindfulness, Nonviolence and the Body.* Life Rhythm, 1990.

Lehrer, Jonah. *Proust Was a Neuroscientist.* Boston: Mariner Books, 2007.

Levine, P. A. and Frederick, A. *Waking the Tiger: Healing Trauma : the Innate Capacity to Transform Overwhelming Experiences.* North Atlantic Books, 1997.

Lewis, T., Amini, F., and Lannon, R. *A General Theory of Love.* New York: Random House, 2001.

Lipton, B. H. *The Biology Of Belief: Unleashing The Power Of Consciousness, Matter And Miracles.* Haye House, 2005.

Llinás, R. R. *i of the vortex: From Neurons to Self.* Cambridge, MA: MIT Press, 2002.

Lowen, A. *Depression and the Body: The Biological Basis of Faith and Reality.* Penguin, 1972.

Macy, J. *Mutual Causality in Buddhism and General Systems Theory: The Dharma of Natural Systems.* Albany, NY: State University of New York Press 1991.

Mahoney, M. *Human Change Processes: The Scientific Foundations of Psychotherapy.* Basic Books, 1992.

Mason, M., Norton, M., Van Horn, J.D., Wegner, D., Grafton, S., and Macrae, N. *"Wandering Minds: The Default Network and Stimulus-Independent Thought."* Science, Vol 315, Issue 5810, pp 393-395, 19 Jan 2007.

Mead, Carver. At http://www.carvermead.caltech.edu/

Mealey, L. *"The Sociobiology of Sociopathy: an Integrated Evolutionary Model."* PhilPapers, 1995. https://philpapers.org/rec/MEATS.

Minuchen, Salvador. *"The Accidental Therapist."* Psychotherapy Networker. Sept/Oct 2009.

Mischel, W. *Personality and Assessment.* New York: Wiley, 1968.

Morales Knight, L. *"Mindfulness: History, Technologies, Research, Applications. Techniques of Psychotherapy."* Pepperdine University, Graduate School of Education and Psychology, 2009. https://allansousa.files.wordpress.com/2009/11/mindfulnessarticleluis.pdf.

Nelson, J. E. *Healing the Split: Integrating Spirit into Our Understanding of the Mentally Ill.* State University of New York Press, 1994.

Newberg, A., D'Aquilli, E.G., and Rause, V. *Why God Won't Go Away : Brain Science and the Biology of Belief.* NewYork: Random House, 2002.

Nisbett, R. *The Geography of Thought.* Free Press, 2003.

Nyanaponika Thera. *The Power of Mindfulness.* San Francisco: Unity Press, 1972.

Ogden, P., Minton, K. and Pain, C. *Trauma and the Body: A Sensorimotor Approach to Psychotherapy.* New York: W. W. Norton, 2006.

Ogden, P. *Sensorimotor Psychotherapy: Interventions for Trauma and Attachment.* New York: W.W. Norton, 2015.

Palmer, Helen. *The Enneagram: Understanding Yourself and the Others in Your Life*. San Francisco: Harper Collins, 1988.

Pandita, S. and Wheeler, K. *In This Very Life : The Liberation Teachings of the Buddha*. Wisdom Publications, 2002.

Panksepp, J. *Affective Neuroscience: The Foundations of Human and Animal Emotions*. Oxford University Press, 2004.

Penzias, A. *Ideas and Information: Managing in a High Tech World*. Simon & Schuster, 1989.

Perls, F. *Gestalt Therapy Verbatim*. Gestalt Journal Press, 1992.

Perry, Bruce. *The Boy Who Was Raised As a Dog*. Basic Books, 2007.

Pinker, S. *The Blank Slate: The Modern Denial of Human Nature*. Penguin Books, 2003.

Porges, S. *"Neuroception: A Sub-conscious System for Detecting Threats and Safety."* May 2004. http://stephenporges.com/index.php/component/content/article/5-popular-articles/20-neuroception-a-subconscious-system-for-detecting-threats-and-safety-

Porges, S. *The Polyvagal Theory: Neurophysiological Foundations of Emotions, Attachment,* Communication, Self Regulation. New York: Norton & Company, 2011.

Ramachandran, V.S. *"Perception of shape from shading."* Nature. Nature Publishing Group, 1988.

Ramachandran, V.S. *Phantoms in the Brain: Probing the Mysteries of the Human Mind*. William Morrow, 1998.

Ramachandran, V.S. *"The Emerging Mind"* Reith Lecture 2: Synapses and the Self. 2003. http://www.bbc.co.uk/radio4/reith2003/

Rhodes, R. *Why They Kill*. Knopf, 1999.

Rich Harris, J. *No Two Alike: Human Nature and Human Individuality*, New York. W.W. Norton 2006.

Rilke, Rainer Maria. *Letters to a Young Poet*. 1929.

Bibliography

Rogers, C. *On Becoming a Person*. Houghton Mifflin. 1961.

Rossi, E. L. *The Symptom Path to Enlightenment: The New Dynamics of Self-Organization in Hypnotherapy : An Advanced Manual for Beginners*. Palisades Gateway Publishing, 1996.

Saxe, Rebecca. *"How Brains Make Moral Judgments."* Ted Talks, July 2009.

Schore, Allan N. *Affect Regulation and the Origin of the Self: The Neurobiology of Emotional Development*. Hillsdale, NJ: Erlbaum Associates, 1994.

Schwartz, R. *Internal Family System Therapy*. New York: The Guilford Press,1995.

Schwartz, J. M. and Begley, S. *The Mind and the Brain: Neuroplasticity and the Power of Mental Force*. Harper Collins, 2003.

Seligman, M. *Authentic Happiness: Using the New Positive Psychology to Realize Your Potential for Lasting Fulfillment*. Simon and Schuster, 2002.

Senge , P. Scharmer, C. O., Jaworski, J. and Flowers, B. S. *Presence: An Exploration of Profound Change in People, Organizations, and Society*. Crown Publishing, 2005.

Siegel, D. *The Developing Mind: How Relationships and the Brain Interact to Shape Who We Are*. Guilford Press, 1999.

Sterling, P. *"Principles of allostasis: optimal design, predictive regulation, pathophysiology and rational therapeutics."* In Allostatsis, Homeostasis, and the Costs of Physiological Adaptation. Eds. Schulkin, Jay. Cambridge, 2004.

Sweller, J. *Cognitive Load Theory*. Springer, 2011.

Taine, Hippolyte. *On Intelligence*. Translated by T.D. Haye. Thoemmes, 1871.

Thurman, R. *Inner Revolution*. New York: Riverhead Books, 1999.

Tiller, W. A., Dibble, W. E., and Fandel, J. G. *Some Science Adventures with Real Magic*, Pavior Publishing, 2005.

Trungpa, Chogyam. *The Lion's Roar*. Boston and London: Shambhala Publications Inc., 2001.

Waldrop, M. *The Emerging Science at the Edge of Order and Chaos*. NY: Simon and Shuster, 1992.

Wallace, A. *Genuine Happiness: Meditation as the Path to Fulfillment*.Wiley, 2005.

Wegner, D. *The Illusion of Conscious Will*. Cambridge MA: MIT Press, 2002.

Welwood, J. *Awakening the Heart*. Shambala Publications, 1983.

Whyte, L. L. *The Unconscious Before Freud*. Garden City, NY: Anchor Books, 1962.

Wilbur, K. *Sex, Ecology, Spirituality: The Spirit of Evolution*. Shambhala Publications, 1995.

Wilson, Edward O. and Holldobler, B. *The Ants*. Belknap Press, 1990.

Wilson, T. *Strangers to Ourselves: Discovering the Adaptive Unconscious*. Cambridge, MA: Belknap, Harvard University Press, 2002.

Wolinsky, Stephen. *The Trances People Live: Healing Approaches in Quantum Psychology*. Bramble Books, 1991.

Made in the USA
Lexington, KY
24 July 2018